Notes from the Other Side of Night

Notes from the Other Side of Night

Juliana Geran Pilon

With a new forward by the author
and an introduction by Mircea Eliade

Transaction Publishers
New Brunswick (U.S.A.) and London (U.K.)

Library of Congress Catalog Number: 2013008858
ISBN: 978-1-4128-5260-9
Printed in the United States of America

Library of Congress Cataloging-in-Publication Data

Pilon, Juliana Geran.
    Notes from the other side of night / Juliana Geran Pilon ; with a new foreword by the author.
        pages cm
    "Originally published in 1979 by Regnery Gateway, Inc."
    ISBN 978-1-4128-5260-9
    1. Pilon, Juliana Geran. 2. Jews--Romania--Biography. 3. Children of Holocaust survivors--Romania--Biography. 4. Romania--Description and travel. 5. Romania--Social conditions--1945-1989. 6. Communism--Social aspects--Romania--History--20th century. 7. Antisemitism--Romania--History--20th century. 8. Political persecution--Romania--History--20th century. I. Title.

DS135.R73P546 2014
940.53'18092--dc23
[B]
                                                                    2013008858

*This new edition of my book is dedicated to my children,
Danielle and Alexander, in the hope that it will help
them love their liberty more and encourage them to
do everything they can to perserve it.
(And remember, grandma Charlotte is watching
out for you from heaven. . . .)*

Foreword to the Transaction Edition

When I first started this diary-memoir in 1975, I had not meant to publish it. So why did I, and why now, four decades later, is it going into yet another edition? By my count, this is the fourth iteration, if we include the never-anticipated 1993 Romanian translation. Contrary to all my expectations, it seems that the recurrent theme of my little book rang true for many readers whose experiences were otherwise quite dissimilar in specific details. That theme revolves around contrast: between innocent childhood and the crisp realities of adult awakening; between a closed and ruthless political system left behind and a risky New World, so bewildering in complexity yet blissfully unaware of its fragility; between home and a new shelter that, no matter how lovely, can never quite shed a sense of exile.

I started writing the book on the occasion of my return, with my parents, to our native Romania in June of 1975—fourteen years after we had immigrated to the United States. At first intended only as a record of my family's experience, I showed my writings to Professor Mircea Eliade and his wife Cristinel. I had first met Eliade as an undergraduate in philosophy at the University of Chicago, having long admired his work on the history of religions. After I learned of his prodigious contributions to fiction, and the Eliades' common love of literature, especially poetry, I was emboldened to share with them my own poems over the years. Cristinel, who was especially taken with *Notes from the Other Side of Night,* persuaded Saul Bellow, who had recently married their friend, Alexandra, to take time from his work on *To Jerusalem and Back* to read my diary-story. Bellow's encouragement and advice proved indispensable in carrying out the many additions and revisions in my original manuscript, essential to a project such as this. Cristinel also persuaded her husband to write a preface to my book in which he acknowledged Hannah Arendt's assessment, which I cite, regarding the tragic fate of Jews at the hands of the Romanian Iron Guard and its sympathizers. Not learning about Eliade's own anti-Semitic pronouncements in his youth until long after his death, I did not appreciate that this may have been his way, however late and insufficient, of atoning.

It was not an easy book to write; it went through countless drafts. Roger, a fellow philosophy student at Chicago and soon to be my husband, who used to charm the Eliades with his guitar (while I danced), helped me immeasurably, criticizing with a sharp eye whenever I drifted into pathos or committed some idiomatic malapropism. I admit to having felt trepidations about the idea of trying to capture a sense of the past and present intertwined. Written to capture both memories and reactions to present events and circumstances, the style could seem uneven, indeed, outright dissonant in places. If so, that was intentional: I wanted to reproduce as accurately as possible the texture of a consciousness shocked into remembrance and recognition, laughing at banality while being terrified by its consequences; conscious of practical issues yet overwhelmed by the tenderness of innocent loves long gone, buried under the lava of man-made cataclysms like so much debris. But if dissonance be the occasional result, it is surely only superficial.

It took me nearly four years to finish the book, but in almost no time I found the ideal publisher—or rather, we found each other. I was thrilled when Henry Regnery, Jr. selected it, alongside a fine book by the (now deceased) French philosopher Raymond Aron, as the inaugural title for the newly revived Regnery-Gateway Publishing Company. Moved by the loving, meticulous care that went into its production, with young Henry overseeing every little detail, I looked forward to many years of collaboration on future projects. It was not to be: Henry never made it beyond 1979. He was one of over two hundred who perished in the runway crash of a DC-10 at Chicago's O'Hare airport while on his way to the convention of the American Booksellers' Association. My little book could not have emerged under more tragic circumstances.

But it did survive, born simultaneously with our daughter, Danielle, that summer. And there was to be a paperback edition, too. A decade on, the Iron Curtain imploded, mostly without violence except for Romania; the West watched with astonishment as tanks ran over innocent civilians on the streets of Timisoara. Then, just before Christmas, the Ceausescus were assassinated after a mock trial. A few months later, television cameras unveiled on film the images of orphans dying in asylums that could only be compared with concentration camps. With all that before them, Americans became interested in Romania, yet they found that few books had been written about this mysterious, fascinating country in the heart of the Balkans. My book was among them.

In short order, with the Cold War's end, many in the West who had never really understood the true face of totalitarianism came to believe that ideological warfare was over for good. Yet, they have learned that human nature changes far less than regimes: the socialist temptation, xenophobia, and groupthink persist to this day. Thus the message of my book, predicated on the importance of individual freedom, continued to be relevant—which led the Sarah Scaife Foundation to award me a grant to republish it. Having appeared in a Romanian translation the year before, the second edition came out in 1994. I am grateful to Jed Lyons of the University Press of America for having kept it in print for the past eighteen years.

Political developments notwithstanding, it is the personal dimensions of my book that most inspired its writing, and I believe these are the main reasons why it continues to resonate. Memories of Romania are, for me, memories of another self, of another mode of life. Walking along the streets of Bucharest and Brasov when I returned, I thought of old wonders, of grandparents brutally lost, slogans no one believed. Having survived quite by chance a holocaust that devoured most of their relatives, my parents persevered for another seventeen years until they were finally able to escape from a new dictatorship, no less repulsive for its ludicrous claim to represent the "people." This dictatorship had made it nearly impossible for my sister and me to learn that we belonged to the ancient, proud people of Jerusalem. While writing the memoir I thought of the many who did not live to testify to that pride and the many whose innocence was no alibi.

And now my parents, too, are no more. How often I want to call my father, not to mention my mother (who remembered better, or at least claimed to do so), to check on one detail or another, only to remember that their deceptively vivid and constant presence within my soul is like the amputee's phantom limb. I know how delighted they both are, wherever they may be, about this new edition.

So, too, for another phantom limb to whom this edition is dedicated: the late Irving Louis Horowitz. Although the book had been kept faithfully in print at University Press of America, I decided to have the rights reverted to me so as to have it reissued by Transaction Publishers, which Irving founded a half century ago. Long under the superb leadership of his wife and now dear friend Mary, this illustrious company has become like family, having published two of my previous books, most recently *Soulmates: Resurrecting Eve*. Though most of Transaction's titles are scholarly, some are addressed to a broader audience. Among the most popular is Irving's own autobiography, first published in 1990 and republished by Transaction in an expanded edition in 2010, not long before he died. Entitled *Daydreams and Nightmares,* the superb little book is both funny and heart braking. Among thousands of brilliant writings on topics ranging from history of modern social theory to genocide and state power, Jewish contributions to sociology, and Latin American politics, as Irving told me, none has received a stronger personal reaction from a broad spectrum of the public. I believe it is—or certainly should be—seen as an American classic.

There is one passage that I found especially arresting. Referring to the way things somehow came together after his leaving the Harlem of his childhood, Irving writes: "The end became a beginning, and the daydreams and nightmares of my Harlem childhood gave way to the more normal existence of youngsters in my station and class. Beyond black and white were boys and girls; beyond good and evil were truth and error." It is no coincidence that Irving's chair at Rutgers University bore the name of the scholar who had explored the banality of evil, Hannah Arendt (and whom I also cite in *Notes from the other Side of Night*). Irving had understood Arendt better than anyone else had. They both saw clearly man's potential for unspeakable atrocities, especially when state instigated and socially condoned. Both understood that freedom is a rare commodity, compassion rarer still.

No poet could have expressed this better than had Irving: "One escapes Harlem the way one leaves a prison: hoping never to return. But the stripes of the prisoner and the Harlemite remain. A spiritual osmosis takes place when the stripes of a confined life are woven into the fabric of mind." Such indelible stripes, different for each of us, inform the texture of all our dreams as we await the final sleep, on the other side of night, where the stars never set.

—Juliana Geran Pilon,
January 2013, Washington, D.C.

Foreword

This diary-memoir was written on the occasion of my
return, with my parents, to our native Romania in June
of 1975. At first intended only as a record of my
family's experience, I showed it to a few friends, among
them Professor Mircea Eliade, my wise compatriot,
and his warm, lovely wife Cristinel. They both urged
me to develop it in book form and adapt it for a wider
audience. Mrs. Eliade's enthusiasm persuaded Saul
Bellow to take time from his work on *To Jerusalem
and Back* to read my book. His encouragement and
advice, as that of so many others, proved indispensable
in carrying out the many additions and revisions required by a project such as this. For its purpose must
transcend the lyrical without compromising it.

The recurrent theme of my book is contrast: from the
other side of innocence, from childhood, from a system
whose ideology prevents trust, to the New World—
paradoxical in its complexity and lack of vigilence. For
me, coming to America at the age of fifteen was also a
transition to adulthood. Thus, memories of Romania
are, for me, memories of another self, of another mode
of life. Walking along the streets of Bucharest and
Brasov I thought of old wonders, of grandparents brutally lost, slogans no one believed.

The personal dimensions of my book, however, must

be set against the larger context. Having survived quite by chance a holocaust that devoured most of their relatives, my parents persevered for another seventeen years to escape from a new dictatorship, no less repulsive for its ludicrous claim to represent the proletariat, a dictatorship that made it almost impossible for their own children to learn that we belonged to the ancient, proud people of Jerusalem. While writing the memoir, I thought of the many who did not live to testify to that pride, the many whose innocence was no alibi.

I offer this book to my new countrymen by way of gratitude for making our freedom possible. It is dedicated to my husband, Roger, an American himself, who is perhaps the main spirit behind the book. Roger has helped me to understand the importance of telling my story, especially at this time, when throughout the West we are seeing a revival of interest in human rights, a renewed concern for genuine justice. At a time when those behind the Iron Curtain who monitor their governments' observance of the 1975 Helsinki agreement are considered criminals, the West can hardly ignore the threat. For surely this is a very small world. And a man's pain is just that, whatever the language of his sorrow, whether Russian, Romanian, English, or Hebrew. It is heartening to see my new compatriots recognize again this elementary though often forgotten fact.

Yet I have no illusions: there will be many who, either from complacency or the dictates of fashion, not to mention ideological myopia, will dismiss these personal stories as so many half-truths. To plead my own case, to fight the perennial though all too human will to believe what contradicts simple evidence, would be both futile and beyond my powers. I will confess, however, that my diary was written not only from a need not to forget but also as a kind of warning: for those who have never left their homeland, for those who have never shed innocence, for those who cannot imagine the loss of freedom, this book is a reminder that there is another side of night.

Finally, a note concerning the format itself. Written to capture both memories and reactions to the present, the style of this diary will inevitably strike some as uneven, indeed, outright dissonant in places. If so, the intention was deliberate: for I have striven to reproduce as accurately as possible the texture of a consciousness shocked into remembrance and recognition, at once protesting and caressing, laughing at the banality of human folly while being terrified by its consequences, conscious of practical issues yet overwhelmed by the tenderness of innocent loves that are long gone — buried in the upheavels of events too violent. But if dissonance be the occasional result, it is surely only superficial. For underlying it all is a simple and harmonious theme, a trust in the stars that manage to shine, in the certain, clear, steady silence behind the confusion that surrounds and numbs us but only for the moment, only for a short while.

Introduction to the Paperback Edition

As my foreword to the first edition noted, this book is a diary-memoir written on the occasion of my return with my family to our native Romania in 1975. It is now a different world. Exactly one decade after the initial publication in 1979, the Iron Curtain imploded; the West watched astonished as tanks ran over innocent civilians on the streets of Timisoara; and just before Christmas the Ceausescus were assassinated after a mock trial. A few months later, television cameras unveiled on film the images of orphans dying in asylums that could only be compared with concentration camps. Many Americans then became interested in Romania for the first time, yet few books had been written about this mysterious, fascinating country in the heart of the Balkans. My book was among them.

Moreover, the end of the Cold War seems to have persuaded some that the ideas of classical liberalism had won, that history had somehow come to an end, that freedom had proven its superiority beyond argument. Yet this is hardly the case: throughout the former Soviet empire the specters of nationalism, xenophobia, and statism loom large. They are present in the West as well, in different forms yet no less dangerous. So the message of my book which is predicated on the value of individual freedom continues to be relevant, and worth restating.

For these reasons, the Sarah Scaife Foundation, which is dedicated to promoting a culture of liberty, saw fit to award the University Press of America a grant to reprint this book in paperback for a wider audience. I am grateful to Dick Larry of Scaife and to Jed Lyons, President of UPA, for making possible the book's second life in the United States.

Coincidentally, it is also being read—for the first time—in my home country. I understand that some of my fellow Romanians feel that my book is valuable not only for having captured a moment in history that left an imprint upon what is happening there today but appears to offer inspiration for renewed dedication to freedom. In truth, I did not believe that these words would ever be read in Romania within my lifetime. Yet in late 1993 an excellent translation was released by Editura de Vest, a publishing house located—fittingly enough—in the Transylvanian city where the Romanian revolution was born: Timisoara.

The book will not please everyone. There are many who minimize or even deny the existence of official Romanian anti-semitism during World War II. Even worse, there seems to be a resurgence of anti-semitism, however subtle. The official adulation of General Ion Antonescu, the Romanian Prime Minister who had collaborated with Hitler, is a case in point. Rabid nationalists will clearly not appreciate my citing historian Hannah Arendt to illustrate Romanian atrocities against Jews.

In this connection, I must draw attention to the introduction written by Professor Eliade. I had known about his early sympathies for a right-wing movement that later gave rise to the fascist Iron Guard. But I did not fully appreciate his acknowledgment of Hannah Arendt's words, in that introduction, until several years after his death, when I learned about some of Eliade's youthful writings that could only be described as anti-semitic. Eliade is evidently himself an example to others who had been seduced by an overzealous nationalism and later found the courage to accept the blemishes of their nation's history. No nation is without sin; my book is meant to recall a horrible episode in order to not forget, and to not repeat the crime. Far from meaning to incite hate, it urges a celebration of life.

This, again, seems to be understood by many of my former countrymen today. I was pleased to return to Bucharest at the time of the book's publication in Romania this past November, when I happened to be in town on the occasion of a U.S. government-funded seminar in civic eduction that I was conducting for the International Foundation for Electoral Systems where I now work as Director of Programs for East-Central Europe, Former Soviet Union, and Asia.

Many of those present that evening were writers who had been unable to publish during the Ceausescu regime, whose words had accumulated within their breasts, men and women exiled like me but worse yet, inside their own land, alienated from their own souls. They thanked me for writing the book to reflect the reality of their lives at a time when such a feat was really only possible from the outside, but instead I could only thank them—for bringing back freedom, for making it possible for me to return, once more, to catch another glimpse of the night I had thought forever beyond my reach. . . .

Yet whatever value the book may have in Romania, its principal audience was and continues to be the American people. For it is in America that freedom found the most solid foundation, based on Thomas Jefferson's Declaration of Independence and a Constitution that codified a classical liberal Bill of Rights. It is here that freedom will have to continue to be defended, and appreciated. Should it wane or even die in America, I am convinced that no one will be safe anywhere. For this reason, I dedicate this new edition of my book to my children, Danielle and Alexander, and their generation, which must relearn the value of preserving freedom if their lives be worth living, and if they are to pass on that legacy to their own children in the next century.

Introduction

I have known Juliana Geran Pilon for nearly fourteen years now. In the beginning I was aware only that she had recently emigrated with her family from Romania and that she intended to study the history and philosophy of science at our university. In the intervening years, however, new dimensions of Juliana's interests and personality were unveiled to me: I discovered that she was a dancer and a poet, and that she was pursuing many other areas of philosophy as well, such as ethics and political thought. In time she offered my wife and me a notebook of her poems, which we read and reread many times, then shared with our friends. Her command of the English language, which she learned only after coming to this country, was truly admirable.

Yet until I read *Notes from the Other Side of Night* I was still only vaguely familiar with Juliana's life before her family immigrated to the United States. The book is a moving record of what she saw on her brief return in the summer of 1975 to the country of her birth and childhood. Above all, however, it is a testimony of memories evoked by that trip, the perceptions of her own childhood woven together with stories of many other lives — the lives of her parents, grandparents, neighbors, and friends. Walking through the familiar scenery of her native home, she remembered streets that are no more, homes and churches that have since been demolished. Yet the hills and forests, the flowers and mountains, the heat of old Bucharest, had all stayed the same . . .

There are scenes in this book that the reader will never forget — such as the celebration of the Passover, performed in the greatest secrecy. And there are fascinating, exceptional characters, admirably portrayed. The three old sisters, for example, who in a little room in a third-floor apartment came to the aid of Juliana's family during their final days in Romania. The goodness and courage of these ladies capture beautifully the memory of those days:

. . . after selling all of our belongings and having not even a bed left, our family slept on the floor of these ladies' apartment. Seven people in two rooms, no mean accomplishment! With love and generosity they helped us leave, gently nursing our parting wounds. To this day, I can still hear the huge clock in that bedroom ticking away very loudly the seconds of our last night in Bucharest. When they saw us off, the eldest of them blessed us with the sign of the cross.

Despite the many tragedies it describes, *Notes from the Other Side of Night* is not a depressing book. Like Nadejda Mandelstam in her *Hope Against Hope,* Juliana writes with a detached, if sometimes melancholy, sobriety, free from melodrama, about events and characters that illustrate Hannah Arendt's terrifying "banality of evil." But Juliana remembers as well those few who managed to remain genuine human beings till the end, defying all danger. And she puts it so well, yet so simply: "there is nothing particularly banal about the good . . ." In essence, what she tells of the survivors, the representatives of a humanity that seemed so natural before the war, is not only deeply moving but heartening and invigorating as well. Rereading the story, one begins, once more, to believe in man . . .

MIRCEA ELIADE

Sewell L. Avery Distinguished Service Professor of the History of Religions

The University of Chicago, April 1979

FOR TWENTY YEARS I had done nothing but prepare for this journey. Not with joy — on the contrary, with anguish. In a dim way I felt where the danger lay: this pilgrimage would be a watershed. From that time on there would be a "before" and an "after." Or rather, there would no longer be a "before." What would be waiting for me when I arrived? The dead past or the past revived? Total desolation or a city rebuilt again and a life once more become normal? For me, in either case, there would be despair. One cannot dig up a grave with impunity. The secret of the *Maase-B'reshit*, the beginning of all things, is guarded by the Angel of Death. One approaches it only at the risk of losing his last tie to the earth, his last illusion, his faith, or his reason.

from ELIE WIESEL, *"The Last Return"*

FLOATING ABOVE THE CLOUDS . . . we could land anywhere. The galaxies don't require passports: round, inscrutable celestial mythology. Each revolution a question: Where does the heart beat? What makes the comet smoke? The puffs of cloud tease the traveler; familiar as breath, they are the testimony of eternity. I try to take them seriously but can't just now; eternity is so irrelevant from this perspective. Going home, the archetypal attempt. The clouds are a pretext — my mind is infested with fragments of memory, swept together in bits and pieces, not even trying to make sense. A patchwork of impressions. Will they fit any of what's left?

I sip my coffee to pretend this is an ordinary trip, from one corner of smug civilization to another. We pass through a dense night, much like the usual but for the proximity of clouds and the curtain of noise. Slowly, light would come, as if to reclaim us. It must be the same sun, the same night. We won't drop into timelessness; I know the signs of voyage. The stewardess smiles, tired. She longs for her hotel bed and a cigarette in peace. Around me, the trappings of reality.

But still a dream: to have returned, after adulthood, to that familiar language — the grammar of fear, the semantics of ideology. No, it's not the same sun, not the

1

same night. How do we spell the new words? They mean what we want them to mean.

Suspended, movement is no longer: instruments are all we have. I search for signs of distance but I find just stars, and they are still. The thick surrounding darkness, the texture of illusion, tempts me to be bold and wonder if our voyage might be taking us to the bowels of the earth, to Dante's ghosts. The stewardess would lead us out like friendly cattle and would name the highlights: "On your left, ladies and gentlemen, is the First Circle. The sinners with some hope." That would be fine, for I would know we had arrived where I had left: among sinners barely aware that desire does not stop with dawn. My compatriots, my old comrades, had not yet mastered their new catechism sufficiently well to forget the distinctions between night and night, blood and wine. Unequipped for the requirements of new salvation, they lay awake with grief, dreaming. A terrible curse, enough to condemn anyone to hope eternal. A kind of drunken folly made them risk their lives on a mere note of sarcasm, a refusal, a demand to leave.

No, this is obviously no ordinary sky: thicker, more ominous, a permanent reminder that seat belts are to be kept on to protect our livers against a tremor within. I close my eyes to listen to the engine covering up the real sounds of night: a hiss of premonitions, the grinding bark of remorse, that murmur of a lust we know as need. The engine seems to laugh at us, monotonous and efficient to soothe as it denies fancy. And it is just as well: my mind should stay clean of mirage if it is to peel off the years gently, accurately.

"Coffee?" the stewardess demands, half-polite, half-resentful. She must think herself too pretty to be stuck in a place like this small old plane with too many seats. I take it she didn't think I was sleeping, or didn't care — her job is to make sure the coffee pot gets emptied. I hand her my cup and thank her but she doesn't seem to hear — perhaps not expecting it, not really believing I need her potion, or just unable to pretend that I am welcome. No hard feelings; I'm tempted to tell her everybody is too pretty to be stuck anywhere, but I don't think she would find that very heartening. I lean back. collecting whatever is left of my thoughts.

My coffee tastes bitter. A bit like expresso, a bit like that hellish liquor we prepared on our trip to the West, our unlikely journey into exile.

The train was probing through the mountains, the wine-colored autumn trees, muttering its old song: clickety-clack, you'll come back, clickety clack-clack don't come back, come back, come back. . . . Our few pieces of luggage nestled on the racks were hopping to the rhythmic noise, as if amused. Most of our belongings had been packed away in a trunk, not to be opened till after we had crossed the mighty ocean. A government list had been issued to remind us of what we could expect to need, though in effect impressing upon us what we must do without.

The Romanian mountains were lavish with foliage, festive for autumn. They made it seem as if we were leaving before a holiday and all the fun was to start after we'd gone. But we knew better.

We watched the scenery, paying no attention to the road-signs — there would be no need to remember. Soon we'd have to learn to spell other,

3

more exotic geographical landmarks. Each foreign word is a lot like the name of a new town: mysterious at first, symbolic of a whole galaxy of relations, it intimidates then becomes as familiar as the inhabitants themselves, friendly and so evident that no other group of sounds seems quite as appropriate.

While passing through the Transylvanian countryside, my mother cried silently, thinking about home, unable still to accept the nomadic turn. No one said anything; we didn't comfort her. Or blame her. Maybe we didn't have the courage to take her pain seriously —each of us had his own terror to confront. Silence seemed better than confusion, even if its price was loneliness —a gamble we were willing to make. Huddled together, we felt less sorry for one another than for ourselves. This was it: the road. And each one of us was convinced he was the least equipped to comprehend it, the most vulnerable.

My sister's small hands were holding mine tightly, as if to make sure I'd stay. She had just lost her small friend: a tiny gold elephant she had been wearing around her neck for years as a charm. My mother had noticed, soon after the train had left the Bucharest station, that my sister was nervously playing with her elephant, teasing it with her tongue. We had forgotton all about it: a small detail with possibly disastrous consequences. Though she could not help turning pale, my mother controlled herself enough to consider the feelings of her eight-year-old and asked very gently to please give her the charm. My sister had obeyed, but a look of alarm indicated that she knew something was not right. "They don't allow these things," my mother explained, almost too quietly to be heard, as much to justify the action

4

to herself as to appease my sister who seemed ready to demand an explanation. But no question was asked, not even when my mother opened the window to toss out the small elephant. The operation done and the window closed, she didn't dare look at my sister. No one quite knew whether the little girl had been upset by her loss — quite likely she too had become numbed by the last three weeks when everything had been sold, given away, or simply thrown out, to accomplish the goal set for us by law: to leave for our journey penniless and unencumbered by material possessions, in true proletarian style.

We were all wearing new clothes, bought in haste with the little money earned from the furniture, lamps, and books we had somehow managed to sell. These clothes were better than what we had been used to, though not by much; at least they were new, and we were hoping to make as good an impression as possible on the people we were to meet "abroad." Headed first for Paris, we had to look presentable. My shoes were a pretty blue, so pretty that I tried to ignore the poor fit (as it was, the salesman put away this pair for me only after we had lined his pockets with a good-sized tip). I kept telling myself they would start to feel better after a bit of walking . . .

We had no one in Paris, only a few distant friends of my parents who had left Transylvania before the war. These Jews, for no obvious reason, had felt safer in Western Europe. We did not have their telephone numbers, but we knew their names and we were sure they lived in Paris. We did not expect them to be well off, and, anyway, we wanted no financial support; but we thought perhaps they would give my father a lead for a temporary job: he

5

spoke French well, and had an aristocratic demeanor —which, we were convinced, would have to help. After we had saved a little money in Paris, somehow, and obtained our U.S. visa, we would join our relatives in Detroit.

These thoughts flashed across my mind repeatedly, like a refrain, yet without the force of reality. We could not absorb it all: only three weeks ago we had no idea that we would leave, at once, allowed at last to cross over to the other side of night. After seventeen years, my parents had become used to the yearly ritual of attempted emigration. They had almost forgotten its eventual purpose, aware only of the need to try again, in a Sisyphean dance with dangerous, taciturn partners who could have ended the charade at any time, no questions asked, no reasons given. A rational end was almost unlikely, under the circumstances; and at first, my parents had refused to believe the little yellow postcard, the famous summons to the police indicating that we could obtain a passport. "A joke, to test our will," they thought, "another cruel stunt."

Their sense of humor sharpened through the years, so long as the border had not yet been crossed my parents were fully prepared for the punch-line. But this state of alert was beginning to wear them out and I could tell that my mother was now watching the copper-colored maples, thinking mostly about autumn. The paradox was slowly paralyzing her usually nimble, practical brain, with its agonizing dialectic: "Do I really wish to leave all this? My familiar train stations; people whose gestures I understand and whose habits speak of regional idiosyncrasies I love to recognize, many of which I

6

share; the hills I climbed as a child, whose forests were my habitat and companion — a kind of green furniture of my memory. . . ." At least I assumed this was what my mother thought about as she quietly cried without making a sound or moving a muscle of her young, tired face. She didn't say, and I didn't ask.

By evening we had reached customs. The wait was hours long, and it seemed like days as we all tried to keep very still, so as not to look nervous when our turn came to be searched. The operation had been started at the other end of the train, so by the time the two young officials came to us they were almost as exhausted as we, which meant — we hoped — that our ordeal would be soon over. One of them was much more aggressive; he turned our clothes upside down thoroughly, expertly, like a surgeon trained to cut quickly to the bone. His "assistant" was more reticent, and looked a bit embarrassed by this superfluous last exercise in harassment. I thought he blushed when our underclothes were being inspected — though it may have been only a reflection of my expectations. It occurred to me as I was watching him that he was probably not much older than I — perhaps eighteen, his moustache so shy one couldn't say whether he was desperately trying to grow it or had not yet started the grownup chore of shaving. Could it be that his seeming reluctance to use his shameful power was beautifying him a bit — enough for my adolescent imagination to be startled to a brief urge for a kind encounter? I wished to tell him it was all right, we didn't mind him any more, we had become used to it, and it would be all forgotten in a few minutes, we would

7

never see him again. At that moment he turned around and, meeting my eyes which did not look away, he stopped his cursory search as if to read me. It may have been a very short glance but I fancied he recognized my friendly intentions. I was not smiling, yet he must have seen that I was not angry with him, that I knew how young and strong he was under his shabby clothes, that I couldn't blame him or anyone at a time like this when we were approaching the long night of dangerous freedom ahead. His look was either gentle or embarrassed, I wasn't sure; he watched me, I thought, with some surprise. "What kind of weasel is it," he must have wondered, "to leave like this, with so little shame in her eyes, so little fear." Uniforms sometimes make one look brave, depending on their symbol. His outfit, however, seemed to camouflage rather than enhance a native wiry wildness. Or so I thought, and I must have shown it. He blushed again and wished to leave. He urged his companion to hurry. After all, our suitcases had been thoroughly ravaged, like a patient after autopsy. Before closing the door behind him, he glanced at me once more, as if to ask forgiveness for an intrusion which had pained him and which was, in any case, beyond his comprehension.

It wasn't long before the train jerked, signaling the long-awaited departure. Without knowing why, I jumped from my seat and went out into the hall, opened the window, and looked outside. Did I want to say good-bye to someone, anyone? To breathe some fresh air before jumping into the tunnel of our journey West, ready to confront that darkness with all the zeal of my ignorance? Or was it merely a

The Carpathian Mountains *(Photo by Paul Grosz)*

subconscious wish to see the young customs official again, to ask him who he was, why he had such a job, or to embrace him — a last seemingly friendly soul from my lovely, ravished home. The train had already started. And as we were leaving, headed toward Hungary, I saw him: standing on the platform, he was watching our train. I was the only person at any window; the other emigrants were obviously obeying the last unwritten law, to give no reason for offense before the flight. As I waved at him, he saw me immediately and smiled. It was a clear, broad, easy smile. A kind of message.

*At last the night had begun. I went back in and
sat down next to my sister. She was almost asleep.
My parents were trying to pack everything back in
the suitcases while attempting to figure out the most
comfortable way to spend the night on the wooden
benches. I closed my eyes and let them take care of
these details, which mercifully distracted them from
the event they preferred not to think about. I knew
that it was my unassigned but implied duty to think,
for all of us: the border.* We are crossing the border.

*The benches turned out to be very hard indeed.
This was the same sort of train we always used to
take to grandma's house. But we discovered that
sleeping on them was more difficult than we had
anticipated. Grandma and Uncle Bandi (my mother's
mother and brother) were in adjacent sleeping cars.
We were unable to afford sleeping cars for ourselves,
but for them it was a necessity: grandma was nearly
seventy and Bandi's paralysis too painful. Actually,
as we found out the following morning, they had not
been able to rest very much either. Not that anyone
complained. The noise, the smell, the constant shaking had conspired to create a romance of transition,
as infectious as it was inebriating. After a while,
lack of sleep made us all feel drugged or drunk or
slightly mad, so that at times the trip became a sort
of hallucination, an uninvited illusion.*

*My father was probably closest to reality, or in
any case seemed most lucid. He was preoccupied, or
tried to be, and relieved too, after signing so many
papers, after bribing right and left — making sure
the amount was appropriate, sufficiently surrepti-
tious, and undisclosed, so as to prevent a last selfish
or envious political stabbing. He must have been*

10

concerned about me and my sister, suspecting secret fear in our excitement, though sensing as well a healthy residue of courage not tested so rudely before. We could tell he was proud of his two little daughters and that made things easier because it somehow gave us a sense of responsibility. But in fact we worried a bit too, not knowing whether his pride was really justified. By way of reassurance, we pretended to be calm.

And tried to eat. We had brought salami and chocolate, for calorie content and also because my father thought we might be able to sell part of it to have a little cash when we arrived in Paris. We needed it for a taxi to take us to some hotel, especially since Uncle Bandi couldn't walk. During our short stop in Vienna, my father proceeded to put his plan to work. He took me along, not so much to help him as to give me the opportunity to see the City of Waltz. Every chance to provide me with an education had to be taken — it was the Jewish way. The plan was carried out: there we were, he with three large salamis on his back, me with my squeaky new blue shoes, getting an education.

The square in front of the station was spotlessly clean, though almost empty of people, it being Sunday. Somehow I had expected fanfare and the commotion of capitalist confusion, so I was rather disappointed. My father, busy with his plan, spotted a coffee house and went in. His excellent German came in handy; the polite waitress understood, nodded, then pointed outside. He thanked her, and seemingly pleased with himself went out in the direction she had indicated. I barely had a minute to wonder at the small wooden tables with neat table-

11

cloths, the two elderly gentlemen engrossed in a deep conversation, and the colorful cakes that reminded me of what genuine hunger was all about.

Still thinking about the cakes, I was quickly taken into a second store, this one far busier. I remember only my concern that I not lose sight of my father, as I had done once in Bucharest when a mere toddler. (Fortunately, at that time I was able to tell a policeman what my address was; now, of course, I had no address.) We were out again within a few minutes, my father two salamis lighter. He had been unable to sell the third one, nor the chocolates. He said, calmly, that he really had not expected to sell them because "the Austrians have excellent chocolates." All the same, he had wanted to try — just in case. "Now we can have mineral water for grandma," he said, meaning that we could go to the train's restaurant like the little old Austrian lady who had just joined our compartment; she regularly brought in sandwiches and delicacies we were too exhausted to envy but hungry enough to speculate about.

As we returned to the train I realized that we must have been gone for nearly two hours, though it seemed like barely ten minutes. My mother said that while the two of us had been away on our commercial spree a young man who spoke Yiddish had come to let everyone know that help was available for Jews like ourselves. He could arrange for us to go to Israel directly from Vienna. We didn't have to travel any further. My mother explained to him that we had a passport for the U.S.A., where her father and several siblings had lived for the past forty years. The young man then told her about HIAS, a Jewish organization in Paris that helps people who are going to America; he wrote down the address. My father looked at it and said: "Now besides money for a taxi we have a place to take a taxi to!" His eyes flickered: not only was there new hope, but he had just made a clever transaction. He was always very satisfied with a clever little idea — in truth, even more than with a clever big idea.

As the train started again, Austria began to reveal its quiet beauty, as if to encourage us further, to help us along our tiring transition. The mountains were less cluttered with leafy beauty than the Carpathians we had just left behind; valleys were broader, homes clean and further apart. Small houses everywhere displayed their fresh laundry innocently, invitingly, drying in the breeze. Just think, an individual family could have a lovely house like that all to itself! The serenity of these immaculate dwellings contrasted sharply with the lurking anxiety ticking like a persistent bomb inside each of us. Why didn't we just stop right here, at the next small village? After all, Austria looked like a free enough country. And then we wouldn't have to go so far, so very far!

The little old Austrian lady got off at Salzburg. She was going to visit her son. Politely, she wished us a good journey. As if we too were on a visit, with a clean bed and a cup of coffee at the other end. Alone again in the compartment, we took out our expresso coffee pot and made enough coffee to boost our energies for about a week. I'll never forget its taste. Bitter and rudely strong, it seemed to shake us from the somnolence of limbo: ready to be careful, ready to think up those clever little ideas that would eventually help us land on our feet, feline and subtle, in a new corner of the Diaspora.

13

I sip my coffee again. It's cold. I notice the stewardess's polite impatience — she must clear the tables before landing. With apologies for my distraction, I hand her the cup and adjust my seat belt. Still pretending, I don't look out the window. It had been easier to come to believe, through the years, that home is where your toothbrush rests, a metaphor at best. And yet, as the plane confronts the ground with the familiar jolt, I awaken: this is my first country, the Socialist Republic of Romania.

The tired Americans parade one by one before the stern customs officials. No one says anything to us, as if our very presence were an implicit insult. Passports are stamped without even a glance. I examine the man who will check my papers: fortyish, suntanned but very tired looking, he barely nods at the people passing by. A stern if not ferocious Cerberus jealousy guarding the dwelling of a caste none of us intends to molest, he will not acknowledge those who enter. His thoughts are made of granite; no one dares to address him unless asked to confirm the trivial essentials in the passport. How little blood must run through the grooves of his spongy brain. . . . Have those circumvolutions of the imagination, thin channels of the mind, dried too soon? And where do they lead? The labyrinth might reveal another House of Shadows, yet Cerberus cannot conceive; he stamps paper automatically. His fixed gaze seems to count corpses — not men, not women. I watch his moist lips, tightened, clenched like a fist. Perhaps he will say something when he notices I was born in Bucharest. Do I hope for a greeting, a smile, a human sign? In vain. Unwise of me to try to forget that these men cannot smile. We are the "enemies," the capitalists whose money they need, whose women they worship, whose luxuries they envy, but whom they must shun. The sunburnt official's lips are cold with secret burning — were he bold enough to awaken, this tamed Cerberus would howl to the skies. But the skies are dark blue, empty of meteors; the price is high for howling. I pick up my bag and pass beyond the gates.

Those gates! How mighty and awful they seem when you happen to be on the wrong side! All the things, small and not so small, they don't allow through! Photographs: twenty per person. No unnecessary trinkets, jewels, or diaries. Not even toys.

No toys. I couldn't rescue my small collection of amusement tools. However few, they had served their purpose as well as any pampered American child's treasure, and even a trifle better.

The first toy I owned was a life-sized dachshund with fur made of burgundy-colored velvet. He wasn't soft enough nor did he look friendly enough to be caressed. But he was held in high esteem and, as I grew older, he participated in my games. Dolls were my favorite playmates, and I had two: Nina, first, whose natural-looking hair became inexplicably more unnatural as I desperately tried combing it to restore its original shine; then Karen, with eyes that closed

15

when she was laid on her back — a feature I had long wanted in a doll. The names themselves are not without significance: "Nina," reflecting my early Russophile brainwashing; "Karen," expressing a barely conscious protest.

Dolls were lots of fun: to make clothes for, to talk to, to put to sleep, to sleep with. I didn't even consider whether they were ugly or pretty, too small or too old. As companions, my dolls were fully satisfying. The idea of throwing them out in favor of more expensive, better attired ones was out of the question. Until my real sister arrived, when I was six, they were my silent, gentle, understanding toysisters.

Besides Daki and the dolls, I had two other toys: my sand pail and Little Bear. The sand pail served for sand dunes we called "castles." Every day I would go to the park across the street to make my little mountains. The sand had to be slightly moist, but not too wet, for the mold to come out right. After eagerly stuffing the pail with the proper ingredient, I would quickly turn it over, then watch the "castle" emerge, very slowly: imperfect every time. Since the next one had to be flawless, the attempts were endless and invariably exciting.

Yet it was Little Bear who became first and foremost among my toy-friends. When offerred to me by close family friends, Little Bear had already spent twenty-five years as companion to their daughters — now married, with children of their own. His most remarkable quality was that, when turned on his tummy, Little Bear growled. Actually, Little Bear was so named only out of affection, for he was truly monstrous — at the time he joined me his

16

size was double my own. Understandably, for quite a while I didn't go near him, just in case he might forget himself and impetuously bite his new owner.

Once I started to trust him, we took dream-trips together. He would lead the way to the glass forests where red-hooded imps lived on raspberries and nectar. We were always welcome in their kingdom, though I never managed to meet their silent, long-bearded monarch residing at the bottom of the lake. I would have had to swim there myself, which would have meant running into frogs and various small monsters. Since Little Bear couldn't swim, there would have been no one to growl at them and frighten the evil spirits.

With such trips, and assured of his gentleness, Little Bear was allowed to share my world. We both knew that the two of us were very different from the way others, who judged from mere appearance, expected us to be. We thus fooled everyone, on purpose cherishing the thought that I was really much naughtier than grownups took me to be, and he very learned. With time, then, Little Bear became more of an equal than a toy — partly, I admit, because of his respectable size.

The authorities, of course, did not allow any objects that might have contained some kind of concealed literature or information to be brought out of Romania, so Nina, Karen, Daki, and Little Bear were left behind. Actually, the authorities had been right: my toys were indeed full of outrageous facts, full of secrets and laughter, and altogether enough joy to amaze any customs officer charged with the job of tearing apart their make-believe bodies, their make-believe souls, in search of forbidden worlds.

The author, age four

It's just as well these men don't smile, for I might smile back, acknowledging an official greeting, a welcome. And I am on no official visit; if no one greets me perhaps I will believe I don't exist, that I am only the memory of one who has died here. (A ghost haunting its home, the never-buried soul unacceptable to the Dark House. I never had my Antigone, ready to find my limbs and risk giving my grave a name. So when I sing, echoing prior harmonies, those I meet have neither eyes nor ears for me — and I, no rest.)

The custom men's faces look green: the sweat, the boredom, has changed the natural color of flesh. Perhaps they are the ghosts, not I. A silly thought. Just because they think of nothing, dream of nothing, wish nothing, their throats are nonetheless clogged.

It is very warm indeed. In the absence of air-conditioning, the heat will continue to haunt me throughout the trip, preventing sleep, creating that halo of sour smell around each person, melting the brain to a point of gentle torpor, more vulnerable to flights of reminiscence.

The smell of dusty, hot Bucharest, the perfume of refuse unwilling to cooperate with the lofty plans of the Euphemists, the new priests. It's the same smell I used to know except deeper, more stubborn, more explicit, hanging low in the air, like an obscenity.

The same trolleys, too, the same buses. Two decades ago they were new — I remember the excitement we felt at the time, riding in "modern" vehicles! (How soon the novelty would fade, with people filling the cars beyond capacity each day.) I'll take the trolley into town, to the hotel.

An unfortunate decision, to be sure: what starts out as an empty car at the airport ends up as a human sardine can within minutes. Again I have the sense of invisibility. The conductoress (lady-conductor? well, hardly a lady) ignores my presence as do the other passengers, except for two young boys who stare at me — a stare that makes me feel quite odd, outright transparent. As the crowd pushes me toward the ticket counter, I ask the conductoress what the fare is. Predictably, she fails to respond. Finally, after I'm already too far from her to be able to pay, she screams: "Can't you talk louder?" A proof of existence! I smile back, but, alas, she isn't looking at me any more. Thus after a momentary lapse into personhood I fall back on my reflections, too exhausted to comprehend why the crowd is squeezing me but doesn't abuse me — all the while screaming at each other, at the additional bunches of people illegally hanging on to the trolley's steps, or at nothing I can identify.

I barely manage to descend at my stop, bathed in sweat and bruised, when it occurs to me that my pretty clothes fit me, my luggage is well made, my haircut in style. How can these people do me the favor of noticing me when they aren't allowed to even imagine me. . . .

Their screams are still within my skull, like the rattle of machine-guns. "The people are one, the country is one!" Slogans are often like expensive placebos: they work when you think they do, no matter. But these drugs are cheaper, and no one needs them. I could be walking through Harlem, so much hate hangs in the air. Do they hate *me?* Each other? No, nothing in particular. Or else it's all self-hate, the foulest kind.

To console and to refresh myself I look for ice cream, those popsicles I used to like so much — always vanilla flavored. Very thin and sufficiently cheap, I used to crave another, and another. I buy one now, wondering if the taste has changed. No; it's the same as it used to be when grandpa brought them to me. And grandpa's popsicles were unforgettable indeed.

I could hear him from afar: grandpa whistling some melancholy Hungarian song, coming from work. He would march in, open his valise full of papers and pencils (very useful for play) and out would emerge those delicious, colorful popsicles, ingheţată pe băţ *("ice cream on sticks") as we used to call them. Bought downtown and kept in grandpa's valise during the bus-ride home, they reached me just about melted but doubly tasty for having just barely survived the trip. Knowing how much I loved them, grandpa bought them enthusiastically every day, without fail. It was the only gift he could afford so frequently.*

Except for one other: his time and his entire soul. It seems that he had never really loved anyone before: not his first wife, who bore him an untamable daughter, nor his present wife — my mother's mother — who wouldn't let him love her. (Was it that she couldn't forgive his Gentile heritage, or that she wouldn't know how to allow anyone to overcome her Gothic metaphysics and impossible dreams . . . ?) Grandpa's first — certainly his simplest — love affair started with the arrival of the smallest member of the family, the eager customer of all the tenderness and wisdom there was to go around.

In the summer, we walked together for miles. Careful to follow my pace, he would hold me tightly like a creature not fully understood, of very delicate constitution — perhaps a kind of soft porcelain — with rules of existence inapplicable to ordinary mortals. He told me stories of bravery with much conviction, as if to inure me to another reality with higher standards, an improbable model of both justice and excitement. How easy it was to believe: his eyes all aflame, he smiled at me with such desire that miracles should happen, sure that indeed they do! I often used to wonder whether his tall, energetic body was

21

hiding one of those mountain heroes whose lives he knew so intimately. Once when he cut down a very large diseased tree I saw him bend over and pause; he noticed me, and said: "We must let the tree fairy run away!" Then he laughed, but I didn't: to think that grandpa could be so mindful of the tree fairy!

Sometimes when we walked, grandpa would describe the flowers, tell their names, when they bloomed, and what their stories were. The story of a flower tells about its origin: for instance, the lonely girl's tears, shed for her dead lover, turned to buttercups; or, from the blood of a wounded doe, trying to save her little fawn, red peonies would spring. The trees as well had very long and complicated stories; their mythical origins explained, the woods would become alive and familiar. Walking with grandpa I felt as fortunate as an initiate in a wild tribe. The mystery of greenery, which I had expected to be both fascinating and awfully difficult to comprehend, was well known to my very own grandpa —for me, a wonderful coincidence.

To rest, we would sit by a brook and grandpa would take out his pen knife, opening it so rapidly, I never knew how he did it; he always frightened me a little, perhaps on purpose. Grandpa would then proceed ceremoniously to cut that thick, Hungarian bacon into small, sweet pieces. With onions and fresh bread, we had our royal feast under the panoply of thick leaves busy gossiping with the breeze. Grandpa loved to see me eat —so I could grow big and strong, like him. (Mother later told me that he used to save up the sugar, the meat, the good food he had been able to buy, and would bring it to us in Bucharest and see my eyes light up.)

"Grandpa"

A child could touch grandpa's spirit and savor it slowly like fresh ice cream. But the seeds of his energy — only after they buried him did I begin to see them, the hope and devilish vitality in his eyes, those eyes that kept telling me to use his love well, to find what he had never known, to be happy, and dance, and tell stories, and eat all the popsicles in the whole world if I wanted to!

The more I eat from it, the less it seems like grandpa's popsicles: nothing but a drop of sugar and some water frozen into a bland, pinkish little finger, mocking me. I lick it with regret, then throw it into a waste basket.

23

Both a stranger and a native, I wander along the streets looking for a friend, or hoping my old self will wake up to me and tell me who I was. Some pedestrian might stop me and explain who he is, who I would be today if I had stayed here.

The little girl in red, with pigtails: she doesn't look about her, sure of her goal. The young woman, prematurely grey, with the vacant stare. They are my own story, retold wordless. Along the boulevard I find pictures of the Leader shaking hands with foreign dignitaries. This new king has recently crowned himself, quite literally: a sceptre was presented to him, as a symbol of rightful power. I am told he has even had a special train built, whose carriages reproduce the interior of an old royal castle. They say tradition is harder to shake than to redefine.

The grey woman talks to me without moving her lips, without seeing me, about her government-issued job she cannot refuse, cannot change; about the room she shares with her old mother who has kidney trouble and no appropriate medicine; about her volatile boyfriend who cannot settle down, cannot marry her because an eagle is tearing at his liver ordering him to breathe, to let go, to start living — and she cannot risk all, for him. The young woman will not smile nor look at me; as I walk along the avenue she is multiplied: the progeny of slogans.

All this dust irritates my lungs. "Pollution," I

think — remembering almost fondly our battles in the States, our reluctance to accept the costs of material progress. No industry is at fault here, just plain old dust, the dirt of hassled Bucharest. The few cars cannot be blamed for the putrid air. (It would be nice to take a shower, but it won't do much good for long, in 95° weather.) Those little cars must be hot inside; and to think how expensive they are (a decade of salary on an average income), and how long a customer must wait to obtain one: after bribing the person who writes up the order, it still takes more than a year to get the car.

A young boy is riding his bicycle alongside the traffic. I notice that there are few bicycles; people must depend on public transportation, they probably work too far from home for pedalling. Undoubtedly the Chinese have it better: those bicycle herds we see on TV captions with little grey men crowding around the American cameras like flies at the light. Everyone is going to a picnic: the People's Picnic! None but the evil-hearted could object to those convict-uniforms, the government-issued jackets of the same noncolor — for the chorus is in tune, the illusion is alive and well.

A bicycle is much like a weapon: you can run with it to save your life, it inspires and creates strength you didn't know you had, it becomes an extension of yourself. As your legs drive it mad, the rhythm catches up with you like a lewd song, in a frenzy of passion, mocking the mechanics of love. Your legs insist on conquering the road — the bicycle is all you've got, so you keep on pumping.

Maybe I'm in love with bicycles — a benign addiction surely. It all started in innocence, with the gentlest of apprehensions.

*After grandpa died, our beautiful garden in Brasov
grew wilder. The flowers were still blooming in
spring, with the tulips in the right place, the lilies,
and the strawberries, but the bushes would stay
untrimmed, the roses would grow more unruly. So
the garden was mourning, too, in its own fashion.
We used the flowers on grandpa's grave, on our way
to the market.*

*The house changed character, too. Part of it had to
be leased, since grandma could no longer afford to
pay rent for both bedrooms, and even if she could,
the state would not allow her and Uncle Bandi to
have more than one room — let alone a whole kitchen
and a bathroom! —all to themselves. As a result,
strangers came to live with them; and during the
summer, as usual, I joined them too.*

*Fortunately, our first neighbors didn't create the
intrusion and bother we had expected. Two army
men, very considerate and kind. One of them, a thin,
timid youngster, smiled often and kept very much to
himself. No one knew his place of birth or whether
he had any family. The other . . . well, the other
caused much turmoil in my little eight-year-old
brain, turmoil that would open a new and exciting
world I was both delighted and afraid to recognize.*

*His name was Kosha —a tall, dark, exceptionally
handsome Hungarian with a beautiful full moustache like a decoration or a bold invitation to drink
or sing or love. Very much a gentleman, polite, his
sense of humor and genuine warmth were barely
stifled inside his officer's uniform. I had never seen
him with a woman —indeed, the very thought of it
bothered me, though I couldn't really tell why. I
would wait for him to come home and then would*

26

try to be close — unobtrusive, but close. He didn't mind; in fact, he played with me often. He once made me a snow man with his bare hands, red with cold. It wasn't just any snow man: he had a big wooden pipe . . . and a dark moustache, just like Kosha!

Then one day Kosha bought himself a brand new, shiny bicycle. I was so visibly taken with it that he offered to take me for a ride. Naturally, I accepted, delighted though somewhat stunned as he put me on the crossbar and started riding. For to my amazement, as soon as I mounted the bewitched vehicle, I lost my sense of time.

It was a warm summer evening. . . . What could have suddenly transformed my small body, electrifying it with expectation? I slowly realized that his face was right next to mine, that my little knees were touching his, that I could feel his breath and his entire body close to mine. We were almost embracing. A few drops of warm rain started to fall, the sun burning low like a coal nearing ashes, and I knew that I was trembling: that I wanted him to hold me like this for a long time, maybe forever, or at least till my body was old enough to want, to give, to change that lonely fear into the desire for a man's touch, a man's lips, a man's need.

It's the heat, I say. People all around me. Some men glance at me. I don't glance back. What is the cause of my revulsion? Latin men with black hair, sunburnt to seem healthy and well fed, they speak my language — I feel a kinship tinged with affection for these hassled husbands and sons of tired, disillusioned women. Is it,

27

then, the impotence they radiate? After all, these are the men who obey the Lie, souls bent out of shape by years of indoctrination, raped by ideology into atrophied robots devoid of sexuality or desire. Their limbs seem limp and unused to love. And the dust that powders their faces — a reminder of the grave, a cosmetic that has already started to eat at their eyes and their lips. (Ideology rapes gang-style, indiscriminately; the orgasm is collective and cathartic, as satisfying as a belch.)

I feel men brushing their bodies against mine, but I can't be sure it's lust — perhaps just another positive reminder of my anonymity. They seem so lost, so spent, unable to want to breathe. I know they have sex, plenty of it: pumping the ecstasy-machine for meaning. And then night obliterates the stink. But come morning they vomit like some pregnant whore heavy with the progeny of a thief. Reality spits in their faces, crushing their genitals. Salute the Chief, kiss the Lie! Kiss it. The Socialist Brothel, brothers! We are all accustomed to make it with bicycles — join the parade! Bring the trombones! We serenade the Red Star! The Hammer and Sickle united in holy copulation. We build socialism with every thrust of virility, predicting the moment of rapture to the last fraction of a second. Surrender your testicles to us and we shall give you pleasure for coupons, to each according to his need, from each according to his seed. (So? Everybody likes a good laugh. Your women do too.) Empty your wombs to the Chief, ladies. The firstborn is a gift to the Cause, and the others a gift to the Hammer and Sickle. All virgins you are, ladies. The Unholy Ghost, each night, touches the magic button: first-rate pleasure, and progeny for the Cause. The progeny of slogans.

28

Be patient, be kind. I tell myself to consider: my friends have survived. As I hold them close, our throats are clogged by the millions of words we must say to each other. But the hotel is completely bugged, secret agents are swarming the streets and coffee shops, and I can't stay at any friend's home overnight because the state doesn't allow it. We walk silently, knowing that my very presence is a risk: Romanian citizens must report having met with a foreigner, and tell what was discussed. But do we really need to talk?

Many of my old friends are gone: I understand that quite a few left illegally, others legally, as I did. It seems that most of my classmates are gone. Of those who stayed, some failed the university entrance exams because they lacked connections, others graduated but were placed in jobs only marginally related to their interests. One hears of many nervous breakdowns.

How old are we, friend? Where do we go from here? Is this a visit or a farewell more final? No, we haven't changed, we look much the same, but we have a curtain of night between us that tastes like raw iron, fresh and hot from the forge.

You haven't done too badly for yourself, considering you are of "unhealthy social origin." I'm sorry about your father dying so suddenly, of a heart attack, the day you took your university entrance exam. You think he was afraid you wouldn't pass — because of your "origin"? He must have been worried that all those piano lessons he had paid for out of his small retirement pension, for over a decade, would have been in vain. He would be pleased to see you are not working your hands to the bone, twelve hours a day, in a factory. You're looking good, friend — considering the exam fever. Would you believe I had a case of that wretched disease myself, even then? Many of us did.

• *Without ever having explicitly discussed the matter with my family, I sensed that I was not of "healthy social origin." I never even asked, almost afraid to find out, about my grandfather on my father's side. I also didn't know at the time that my father had been placed in various risky, low-paying, grueling jobs, in part because of an accusation, which he had no power to refute, that his father had owned a large piece of land before the Communist takeover. The accusation was particularly ludicrous in view of the fact that before 1945 Jews were not allowed to own land. Actually, as my father told me only after we left Romania, grandfather had been no great capitalist threat to class struggle, living as he did on his reasonably taxed salary as chief accountant of a lumber company.*

I had not paid much attention to the matter of my "origin," really, until it became clear that one could be denied entrance to high school (and of course to college — that was common knowledge) on the basis of one's social background. I remember how I first realized the significance of this policy. On the fateful day of "the results," a friend of mine, a very serious, studious girl, the daughter of a Jewish dentist, was shocked to find that her name was missing from the list of students admitted to high school. She had always been in the top one percent of her class and had taken the week-long exams calmly and confidently. As she read the names of "winners" posted at the school (it did not need to be confidential — privacy was just barely legal because theoretically dispensable), failing to find her own, she froze in disbelief. As I looked at her afro-curly blond hair defiantly untamed by the required white headband, her lips pressed together tightly, I could tell that the bright mathematician saw her future clearly: tedious, sometimes backbreaking factory work for the rest of her life. There were no second chances. (The barrage of indoctrination had not managed to make manual labor the desideratum our leaders hailed it to be; for one thing, we couldn't help seeing that they themselves no longer engaged in it.) My friend had always seemed too dedicated and too conscientious, almost sad; her expression was the same now, as she stared at the bulletin board, as she realized — perhaps for the first time — that studying hard had not mattered in her case. Though I sympathized and wished I could help, I too said nothing and found myself thinking more about my own examinations, coming up the following year. "Her parents must have asked to emigrate," I thought to myself, not knowing that I, not she, was in that situation: my parents had carefully concealed it, to save me the anxiety.

From such threads was sewn the texture of apprehension that covered us all, Jewish children of ex-tailors, shoemakers, small shopowners, ex-civil servants and other brood of the petty-bourgeoisie, who proceeded to study especially hard. It was possible

31

to imagine that you would make it, that justice does exist somehow, and you could persuade yourself that every one who seemed to be unfairly persecuted did in fact conceal some sort of social crime. We therefore agreed to pretend that we were learning humanities and history, and we memorized the stock "introductions" and "conclusions" to be attached to every term paper. Fortunately, the same phrases could be used over and over again — the difficulty lay in making them sound different without in fact saying anything new. Most of us caught on to the mechanics so well that we didn't even see the words: they had become a sort of code, a song, a pagan litany compromising no one because no one took it literally. Lying implies believing, and there was no danger of that. Almost as innocently as our prehistoric relatives, we had grown up in a vacuum of information, and learned our catechism for mere survival. Studying became no less mechanical than jumping rope (except for the by no means inconsiderable risk of being hanged). Our textbooks were full of gaps; we had become cynical about "facts," and no longer needed them. At least we knew what they didn't mean — and negative definitions would have to do.

Take the periodic reduction of prices. As soon as the newspapers announced another drastic improvement in the economy, we could be sure to see the cost of motorcycles drop from the equivalent of a couple of years' toil to that of, say, a mere one year and ten months. At the same time, a pound of beef would be up from half a day's salary to three-quarters of a day. Using her old-fashioned economic intuitions, my mother tried to look at the bright side:

the price hikes might help with the shortage of meat. But, to no avail; our religiously quotidian trips to the butcher resulted in the same disappointing ration of one fatty pound every three weeks or so. (Mysteriously, neither did motorcycles multiply on the streets of the People's Republic.)

Another problem with definitions arose at the produce market. Who were the wretched "owners of private property" we all had to hate as "enemies of the people"? Could they possibly have anything in common with those sickly old women, their clothes torn and teeth missing, who came each day at five in the morning to sell eggs, and vegetables, and chickens? They had no shoes —only thin sandals —and usually no umbrellas. (Maybe they didn't want such amenities. Maybe the rain felt good to them as it poured: rain is a peasant's friend and ally.) Why were we supposed to await their dissolution, the total triumph of socialism? The vegetables tasted better, their chickens were cheaper than in the state stores, and at least they had eggs available. What of that?

I didn't hate them, and didn't hope for their "dissolution." In the final analysis, one can do without facts, not to mention definitions. We therefore thought little, and explained less. Somewhere there lurked a conviction — generated, perhaps, by an inability to imagine unmotivated and senseless evil — that there had to be a reason for the curtain of misinformation separating us from our own perceptions, a reason why some of the brightest students were treated with cruelty, a reason both virtuous and inevitable. So we each decided to keep hoping, appeasing our anxiety with a secular version of Pascal's wager, which went something like this: "What do you lose by working? Only if 'they' are altogether against you is it futile to be a good student; if a mere cloud hangs over your head it might help to earn the best grades." It seemed sensible enough; convinced, I worked hard, keeping the chills of apprehension even from myself.

Some of my colleagues, I noticed, were less prudent. The top prankster in the class, Otto Waldman, made a point of ridiculing the political zeal of the more blatantly demogogic among our teachers. It seemed to me that Otto was almost deliberately careless in his disrespect —why, he was just about asking for his consistently low grades in Citizenship (or, as it was called in our country, "Behavior"). True, my own mark had been lowered once, too, for an offense I considered insignificant: I had refused to pull all my hair back under that hated white headband, leaving a few unruly curls on my forehead in defiance of our political leaders' aesthetic judgments. But after I realized the ominous implications of such sanctions, I dutifully complied with the required puritanism. Otto, on the other hand, became more belligerent and determined as time went on, indeed, more subversive as well. "They tell us about capitalism," he said to a few of us, "but did you see what good pencils they make? and how good their erasers are?" It would have been easy to denounce him: the files are secret. Many probably did, since all anti-socialist activity had to be reported, and failing to do so was itself a crime. But then why did he continue to court trouble? We couldn't understand Otto: his father had an important job as director of the *National Bank, and Otto would have had an easy time taking advantage of all his privileges. Yet he was restless. He kept playing the fool, and harping at facts he couldn't reconcile with what we were told, facts most of us had decided to ignore. Who knows, maybe he just felt that all Jews would "get it" some day anyway.*

Or maybe his strikingly attractive, olive, Semitic face and pitch-black curly hair caused that boldness of his, found only in a natural elite. The same boldness may have prompted his asking me, one evening, to love him; I laughed, thinking he was engaging in another of his facetious pranks. It is nevertheless strange how I did not stop to consider that he was not smiling in the least. Otto operated by rules foreign to the rest of us. I would have been unable to begin to learn them, or so I thought.

Though Otto was anomalous in flaunting his resistance, those of us whose "origins" were somehow "unhealthy" slowly came together in a group that was defined by a sense of general skepticism. In truth, at first I resented having to be a part of it: I found myself protesting that my social background should not be held against me, for accidents of history must surely be irrelevant to the worth of each individual. But gradually I began to appreciate the therapeutic value of detachment and humor, and the distinct advantage of feeling estranged from people who made it difficult for me to learn simple, interesting "facts," to learn about my gentle, hardworking Jewish grandfather. "A stranger among so many strangers!" I thought. Why, a whole country of strangers. . . .

More raspberries? Yes, thank you. I haven't eaten in a while. People give me whatever they have and now it is the fruit season. These raspberries were bought at the same market located in the center of Bucharest where my mother and I used to queue up for our daily bread and margarine. The old women with torn sandals are still there. Not much is changed. Fruit and vegetables are still unavailable out of season. I ask if two eggs still cost the same as a pound of bread — about an hour's wage. "About." And what about beef? "We have cheese," I'm told, "but please don't ask about food. We

The author's paternal grandfather

eat." What should I ask, then? I need to know. What can I send them from America, after I return? "Send us books," comes the unlikely answer. Why, has everyone become politicized? How can you possibly want books, I ask, when you can be imprisoned for it? No, they don't imprison us for *all* books. Send us books about Mexico in the Middle Ages, about beads and porcelain, about ancient religions, about mountains, and ancient languages, maybe some novels too, and poetry.

I listen, not quite believing their request. The tablecloth has been mended in a dozen places, the furniture is pre-revolutionary, and there are not enough plates to go around. Yet they are asking for books. I look more closely: a dozen young people have gathered to meet me, the few who are left from my class of about fifty. When I first walked in, there had been a sign of excitement — subdued, but unmistakably friendly, Still, they asked no questions, seeming reticent if not afraid. I had wondered why, and thought perhaps they were either ashamed to have me shatter their carefully spun illusions or worried that I might remind them of the spoon-fed nonfacts protecting them from remembering how trapped they all are. But this could not have been the explanation. For it occurred to me that today these people are far better informed: they have access to the *Herald Tribune,* many read French and German newspapers brought in by tourists or sent by friends, some have even seen *Time* ("a leftist magazine, isn't it"), and listening to Radio Free Europe is common practice. I suspect, in fact, that they ask little because they already know my answers to the most important questions. Besides, in any group there must be informers.

Of course: our meeting will undoubtedly have to be

reported. With so many gathered, it cannot stay secret; it is therefore best to keep it very low key. (Note: in this diary, too, I must refrain from recording anything that the Secret Police might be able to trace to a specific person.) So I ask most of the questions. It is less risky.

I wish to know which of our classmates have left the country. I am told that Irina Loebl (the daughter of a writer and a well-known actress) married a foreigner, which afforded the easiest opportunity to leave for the West. Irina's mother committed suicide shortly afterward. Calin Manoilescu, who used to be a shy, gentlemanlike young boy, is now in Paris. Our exaggerated puritanism had had an opposite effect on him and his incontinence became legend long before he left the country to join his relatives abroad. And Otto? Otto Waldman emigrated with his family — first to Israel, now they say he is in Brazil. During his last years in Romania he had been increasingly harassed for his insubordination.

Many more have gone. Reasons are not given, nor do I need to ask. Of those who are present, most still live with their parents, whether or not a spouse has joined them. I can find them at the same address they had fourteen years ago. (I discovered that this was usually not a sign of excessive attachment to the original atomic family but an arrangement of mutual benefit. The parents could thereby avoid having to accommodate total strangers who would move in, under state authority, to take the space of the child who had moved out, while the young ones would be spared the anxiety of being assigned to live in another city, the long waiting period preceding the assignment, the inconvenience of new buildings carelessly constructed, and the rent which for most newlyweds was exhorbitant.) Most of them cannot afford children. The high "childlessness" tax (to be paid, incidentally, by the unmarried and the infertile as well) has a paradoxically contraceptive effect, making it harder for a couple to save any money for a future family. And why breed more soldiers for the regimented society? The Führer be damned.

While these people ask for books, they are remarkably resigned. For the past two years it has been nearly impossible for them to travel abroad, even to other socialist countries, yet there are no complaints. At least once a week or so they are all required to march in the streets to hail their self-styled prophet returning from another Third World campaign for socialist equality (a mask of "independence" suits him well, they say, in his dance to the Soviet drum), but no complaints. Censorship of the arts has tightened since the new cultural revolution (Chinese style; we learn from them all), but there is nothing to say.

I wonder which of them is an informer. I finish the raspberries, and promise to send books. My friends, of course, aren't hungry.

I walk slowly from my old kindergarten toward my house. "My house" I used to call it, though all that belonged to us was a rented apartment on the third floor of a grey inconsequential building.

The only redeeming feature of our modest dwelling was a tiny balcony overlooking the world. Since the railing was rather low and dangerous for a small creature like myself, my father "fenced it up" with a wire screen. To improve its appearance and detract from its prison-like quality, we planted morning glories. Every morning I would go to check whether a new flower had appeared to greet me. If I found one, it seemed like an omen, a promise of a whole day's happiness. The dead flowers were not removed until they were altogether dry — but even then, instead of mourning them, I turned them into an object of play. My mother had taught me to take them by the petals, blow into them like a balloon, and "pop" — their requiem would turn into a gentle laugh.

The balcony was my little kingdom in the city. I could sit for hours watching the people and the occasional cars. Frail housewives carrying those heavy blocks of ice in the summer, enough to sustain the ice boxes for a day or two. And tramways passing noisily by the house. I eagerly waited for an occasional spark: the electric shock from the meeting of cable and car, which to me had all the magic of fireworks. The tramway seemed driven by a demon: approaching with deafening noise, always in a mad hurry, desperately chasing its destination.

When summer was very hot, mother would fill the hole that helped drain the balcony, and bring a few bucketfuls of water from the house, to create a mini-swimming pool a couple of inches deep. Those were delightful times, rubber boat and all! It didn't take much to imagine the sea, the very ocean, complete with mermaids! When mother came to fetch me at the end of my sloppy day of splashing about the balcony, she found a happy, filthy, rosy little piglet drunk with heat, clearly oblivious to manners and refined taste!

In spite of its bland, indeed outright boring appearance, our apartment building was actually a Gothic castle with its share of grotesque stories and ghostly characters.

The strangest was our old weaver: he lived in the garage, an uninsulated hole on the ground floor of our building. In this unorthodox dwelling were found a bed and a huge working table: the old man made feather and wool quilts and mattresses. He had no family, and perhaps no thoughts, for I never heard him say one word. In the morning he would loudly raise the garage door for the sun's rays to decorate his humble headquarters, and either he worked at his long table or else sat outside, on the thin turf of grass in front of the building, combing wool, slowly, deliberately, with a stoicism approaching abandon. And what a picture he was: a saintly-looking man, perhaps seventy years old though very sturdy, with a head full of hair and a long lovely beard — both glowing like a halo, the color of the yellowish white wool rocking in his rudimentary machine. A relic worthy of a Rembrandt. We often sat together, but he said nothing. No one knew his name. The god of weavers, perhaps.

The moldy basement housed an improbable number of people. One family with a child lived in two rooms, each the size of a queen-size bed. The woman who did our laundry (we had never even heard of washing machines in those days) occupied a room big enough for a mattress and a small table.

41

There were others too, bachelors, living in the base-
ment cells —and whenever I went down there I felt a
bit guilty: it was always so damp and smelly, unfit
for man. No one complained, but the outrage hung
in the air as thick as the odor. Of course, these
people were all employed, on minuscule salaries.
The proletariat. If this be their dictatorship, alas . . .

The building proper housed people who de-
nounced each other, hated each other, shared kitch-
ens and bathrooms. The second floor —the heart of
the building (or, rather, its spleen) —housed an ex-
plosive bunch: a colonel with a wife and young son
in one room; an old lady, formerly upper class, in
another room; and a childless couple in the third. All
of them cooked in the same kitchen and took turns
in the only bathroom: their fights were understand-
ably bloody. (Andrei Sinyavsky's short story "Ten-
ants" describes this kind of situation quite aptly.)
The colonel's wife was the building informant —she
reported to the secret police. (Almost every house
has at least one such person whom others know to
be an informant, though the countless spies who are
not suspected are, of course, far more dangerous.)
The top items to be reported included: (a) who is
visiting whom, (b) who seems to be dissatisfied with
his lot in life, and (c) does he appear to be blaming
the government for it? My parents didn't complain,
so categories (b) and (c) were easy to avoid. But on
one occasion my grandmother who lived in Brasov
visited us for a couple of days, and within a few
hours a secret police officer was knocking at our
door to find out whether she was registered with the
city administrative offices as a guest, in line with
regulations. (House spies worked fast!) Fortunately,

she was. Unfortunately, she visited the Israeli Embassy on the following day, to try — however hopelessly — to find out about the status of her request to leave the country. As a result, my whole family, as well as the people who visited us, were followed day and night for the next two months. (My parents told me about this incident only after we left Romania, so at the time I slept well while they kept vigil expecting the worst.) How naive of us to think that her trip would leave no mark. Our house was no refuge.

On the first floor were two separate apartments of one room each. One was rented to a woman of uncertain age, heavily made up, sensuously overweight, who seemed to entertain mostly men. Next door lived a middle-aged lady doctor who performed illegal abortions. (I have no doubt, in retrospect, that the proximity of these two characters was altogether coincidental.)

On the third and last floor was our two-room apartment, adjacent to another slightly smaller one but which, thank heavens, had its own bathroom and its own kitchen (no matter how tiny — nothing fit in it besides a small stove and a thin cook.) The tenants of this dwelling were not in the least ordinary: two ladies — one in her late nineties, her sister, late eighties — plus the former's daughter, over sixty; all three were in perfect health and very aggressive, going to concerts and plays every week. Formerly upper-middle class, the ladies appreciated "the finer things in life." The eldest was particularly energetic: she would discuss politics, science, literature. She even kept up with the changing trends in education. A high school mathematics teacher in her youth, she especially wanted to know about "the new methods" of teaching geometry — it delighted her to hear that they hadn't changed. (I am told she died at the age of a hundred and five, in her sleep, without having lost any of her intelligence or wit.) Her "kid sister" (as she used to call the eightyish youngster) was very quiet, enamored of solitaire: whenever I came for a visit she was engrossed in her card games. As for the youngest of the three ladies, she became my mother's most trusted, loving friend over the years. I remember we used to join the neighboring trio sometimes for classical music concerts broadcast on the radio — their set was better (though much older) than ours. These ladies would listen with such religious ardor, such appreciation, it made me happy just to be with them.

And then there was the unique memory of our last days in Romania when, after selling all of our belongings and having not even a bed left, our family slept on the floor of these ladies' apartment. Seven people in two rooms, no mean accomplishment! With love and generosity they helped us leave, gently nursing our parting wounds. To this day, I can still hear the huge clock in that bedroom ticking away very loudly the seconds of our last night in Bucharest. When they saw us off, the eldest of them blessed us with the sign of the cross.

As I approach the building a chill comes over me: how run down it is! The grey walls are much darker now. I am angry with myself: why am I here? Why did I come to see it? What do I expect to find, anyway?

As I stand looking at the building, ready to turn

around and leave, I hear a gypsy woman calling to me: "Hey, come here," she says with the characteristic directness of her people. "I remember you. You used to live here." Stunned, I look ... and recognize her! I never knew this woman's name, we never really met, I only used to buy flowers from her. The same missing tooth, the same enormous filthy skirt; braless and brazen, ageless, the gypsy woman sells flowers as she did so many years ago, as most of the women of her race do in Romania. She is still selling on the same corner. But how could she remember me? I don't ask, she just does. There is nothing to tell — her life is the same, there is nothing for me to say. I buy flowers from her; she sells them, as mechanically as ever, bargaining of course. I pay as much as she wants. She asks no questions of me either, she never asks.

I walk away from my former home. What could have brought me here? It's just another dwelling in the city, another of Dracula's modern day castles where, periodically, the tenants' blood is sucked out with coarse, socialist syringes. (A red flag is most appropriate, Count!) Each body recovers its vital fluid, manufacturing it anew from starch and vinegar, but the memory of the last sucking leaves the veins more limp, more susceptible to hemorrhage. In these dwellings, people's dreams are full of bats: red bats, flapping their wings like flags. (Since the cross has been outlawed, they say, there is no protection.) Haunted apartment buildings — were these but prisons! Nothing can keep away thirsty bats; the Count drives them mad, mad. Behind their thin curtains, the tenants wait, necks exposed, for the Medieval ritual: long live the Hammer and Sickle! Transfusions for the good of the Cause!

What on earth do I expect to find? Admittedly, at the

45

time I lived here I didn't know about the side of night that belonged to the vampires — my tender arteries filled with fresh thin liquid had been molded to withstand attack, anesthetized through my parents' constant concern that I not perceive. Nevertheless, in the midst of the antiphonal propaganda, a thin Semitic melody — below the threshold of sound, yet indelibly imprinted on the neurons of my core — was weaving its way skyward. My family used to celebrate our *special dinner* most unobtrusively but with the same determination that kept this resilient people alive since biblical times.

Although it wasn't Sunday, my father didn't go to work. I liked the day because we could spend it together and we would have a special dinner, with food we could not always afford. My father would bring home some delicious biscuit called "pasca," packed in a box with strange letters on it. He would buy it in an unusual place, a dark little room in a building quite far from where we lived. The room was not at all like a store —only boxes of this biscuit everywhere —and the people were all very quiet, hardly looking at each other. My father would pick up the package quickly then leave, holding me by the hand very tightly, as if afraid he might lose me. For the special dinner we also had a large piece of meat for a main course, and even wine. I really would have liked to know what this festivity was all about.

My sister was curious about the funny letters on the matzo box, so my father told her it was Chinese. Zionism, like fascism, was considered illegal; it would have been dangerous to let her know there was "Zionist" writing in our house, since she was too small to remember what not to say. I trustingly, if unimaginatively, took the "biscuit" to be some kind of especially nourishing imported food, though it did seem strange that we ate it only once a year. "Maybe that's the only time it's available," I reasoned, well versed in socialist rules of supply and demand.

I admit it did seem a bit strange that my father did not go to work for a whole day, but I didn't demand any explanation. Since it was not always on the same date, I couldn't consider it a regular holiday like November 7, the anniversary of the Soviet Revolution. I did notice it was a spring-time celebration, and wondered whether such a special dinner was possible only when "pasca" was sold. But why make a big fuss over a mere cracker? I might have understood it better had we celebrated some fancy desert, or tangerines, but "pasca"?!

Yet undoubtedly a holiday it was: my mother risked her best white tablecloth, so easily stained by diners like me and my sister, whose appetite was exceeded only by our oft-demonstrated clumsiness. Scrubbed and starched, the white linen seemed stiffly uncomfortable with us children, its own venerable identity reflected in an elaborate (and very difficult to iron) pattern of three letters. My mother had told us it was a "monogram" — which reminded me of "telegram = a very important message." What enigma did the tablecloth conceal? Maybe it could not be revealed to just anyone, such as mere kids. The same cipher appeared on the napkins, providing one more (if not the only decisive) reason my sister and I consistently shunned them.

And then, of course, the curious candles. We especially liked the way they were lit: three little candles placed close together to be kindled at once. It made for an unusual effect. (I assumed there had been no larger candle in the store, and this was my mother's way of improvising. How such practical explanations eliminate the need to wonder about symbol. . . .) Their peculiar smell stayed with us throughout the special dinner, blending with the others, yet never fully obliterated.

What smells they were, too! First, it is true, we had to finish some odd appetizers: radishes (with stems; my mother never allowed it on other days . . .), parsley, which I pretended to eat but managed to hide under my spoon when no one was looking, and part of a boiled egg (divided in four so that everyone could have some; usually my sister and I were given all of such scarce wholesome food). Then the real feast began. Chicken soup with several whole dumplings, richer than usual. And then a whole chicken, for only one meal, prepared with wonderful spices and a thick sauce. (My mother was an expert at using one chicken for at least three meals; but this time she really splurged!) Last came the biggest treat: dessert. My sister and I were given a small bar of chocolate each — the only time we had it, the whole year. Knowing how expensive it was, we munched on it slowly, waiting for it to melt from the heat of the tongue. I remember now that we never offered even a bite to my parents. It seems that we simply assumed grown-ups don't like the same sorts of things kids do. After all, they drank that wine we didn't particularly care for, and they seemed to enjoy it a lot. Remarkable, what rationali-

zations we selfish little creatures were able to believe.

It would have been impossible, of course, to overlook the importance of the special dinner. But it was especially difficult to do so in light of my father's peculiar behavior at the table. Before the meal, and also at the end, he would read from a book something we couldn't understand. He didn't seem to be addressing anyone, just whispering to himself. The book, I noticed, was full of the same kinds of letters as the ones printed on the "pasca" box. I was so curious about the coincidence, I kept hoping to get the book off the shelves and examine it at my leisure for some clue. Since my father had many unusual volumes, including some leather-bound ones which, he said, had "Gothic letters," I was already used to eccentric reading tastes. But why could I never find that *book? Somehow I knew there had to be a reason, and asking about it would not have been wise. Then one day, very unexpectedly, part of the mystery unraveled. While searching through an old box at my grandma's house I found a magnificent tome, with golden-edged pages, its cover made of thick ivory. As I opened its finely sculpted clasp, I froze: there they were, the same letters. I ran to grandma to ask what it was, this lovely book. "Why, the Bible!" she answered, and put it away immediately, in a safer drawer, which she locked twice. I had never seen a "Bible," but I knew it was some kind of forbidden object. "It probably shouldn't be translated," I thought. But what would my father be doing with a book written like the Bible? And why the strange writing on that biscuit? Perhaps it was best not to wonder.*

So I did not know that what my father said as he drank the wine was this:

בָּרוּךְ אַתָּה יְיָ אֱלֹהֵינוּ מֶלֶךְ הָעוֹלָם, שֶׁהֶחֱיָנוּ וְקִיְּמָנוּ וְהִגִּיעָנוּ לַזְּמָן הַזֶּה.

(Blessed art Thou, O Lord our God,
ruler of the world,
who has kept us alive, maintained us, and enabled
us to reach this occasion.)

And as he uncovered the matzo:

הָא לַחְמָא עַנְיָא דִּי אֲכָלוּ אַבְהָתַנָא בְּאַרְעָא דְמִצְרָיִם. כָּל דִּכְפִין יֵיתֵי וְיֵיכֹל. כָּל דִּצְרִיךְ יֵיתֵי וְיִפְסַח. הַשַּׁתָּא הָכָא. לְשָׁנָה הַבָּאָה בְּאַרְעָא דְיִשְׂרָאֵל. הַשַּׁתָּא עַבְדֵי. לְשָׁנָה הַבָּאָה בְּנֵי חוֹרִין.

(This is the bread of distress
which our forefathers ate in Egypt.
All who are hungry — let them come in and eat.
All who are ready — let them come in and celebrate
*   the Passover.*
Now we are here.
Next year may we be in the land of Israel!
Now we are slaves.
Next year may we be free men!)

And why do we eat the bitter herbs?

מָרוֹר זֶה שֶׁאָנוּ אוֹכְלִים, עַל שׁוּם מָה? – עַל שׁוּם שֶׁמֵּרְרוּ הַמִּצְרִים אֶת חַיֵּי אֲבוֹתֵינוּ בְּמִצְרַיִם, שֶׁנֶּאֱמַר: וַיְמָרְרוּ אֶת חַיֵּיהֶם בַּעֲבֹדָה קָשָׁה, בְּחֹמֶר וּבִלְבֵנִים, וּבְכָל עֲבֹדָה בַּשָּׂדֶה; אֵת כָּל עֲבֹדָתָם אֲשֶׁר עָבְדוּ בָהֶם בְּפָרֶךְ.

בְּכָל דּוֹר וָדוֹר חַיָּב אָדָם לִרְאוֹת אֶת עַצְמוֹ כְּאִלּוּ
הוּא יָצָא מִמִּצְרַיִם, שֶׁנֶּאֱמַר: וְהִגַּדְתָּ לְבִנְךָ בַּיּוֹם הַהוּא
לֵאמֹר: בַּעֲבוּר זֶה עָשָׂה יְיָ לִי, בְּצֵאתִי מִמִּצְרָיִם. לֹא
אֶת אֲבוֹתֵינוּ בִּלְבָד גָּאַל הַקָּדוֹשׁ בָּרוּךְ הוּא, אֶלָּא אַף
אוֹתָנוּ גָּאַל עִמָּהֶם, שֶׁנֶּאֱמַר: וְאוֹתָנוּ הוֹצִיא מִשָּׁם, לְמַעַן
הָבִיא אֹתָנוּ, לָתֶת לָנוּ אֶת הָאָרֶץ אֲשֶׁר נִשְׁבַּע לַאֲבֹתֵינוּ.

(It is because the Egyptians embittered
the lives of our fathers in Egypt.
As the Holy Scriptures say:
"They made their life bitter with hard labor:
with bricks and mortar, with all kinds of work in the
      fields,
all of this forced labor being rigorous."

In every generation a person must see himself
as though he, personally, came out of Egypt.
As the Holy Scriptures say:
"You shall tell your son on that day
'This is because of what the Lord did for me when
I went forth from Egypt'."
It was not only our forefathers
that the Holy One, blessed be He, redeemed,
but He redeemed us, too, with them.
As it is said:
"He took us out from there,
in order to bring us hither and to give us
the Land which He had promised to our fathers.")

My sister and I didn't like the parsley. My parents
   ate it slowly, as if savoring each leaf.
The prayers went on:

51

אָהַבְתִּי כִּי יִשְׁמַע יְיָ אֶת קוֹלִי, תַּחֲנוּנָי; כִּי הִטָּה אָזְנוֹ
לִי, וּבְיָמַי אֶקְרָא. אֲפָפוּנִי חֶבְלֵי מָוֶת, וּמְצָרֵי שְׁאוֹל
מְצָאוּנִי, צָרָה וְיָגוֹן אֶמְצָא. וּבְשֵׁם יְיָ אֶקְרָא: אָנָּא יְיָ
מַלְּטָה נַפְשִׁי! חַנּוּן יְיָ וְצַדִּיק, וֵאלֹהֵינוּ מְרַחֵם. שֹׁמֵר
פְּתָאיִם יְיָ, דַּלּוֹתִי וְלִי יְהוֹשִׁיעַ. שׁוּבִי נַפְשִׁי לִמְנוּחָיְכִי,
כִּי יְיָ גָּמַל עָלָיְכִי. כִּי חִלַּצְתָּ נַפְשִׁי מִמָּוֶת, אֶת עֵינִי מִן
דִּמְעָה, אֶת רַגְלִי מִדֶּחִי. אֶתְהַלֵּךְ לִפְנֵי יְיָ בְּאַרְצוֹת
הַחַיִּים. הֶאֱמַנְתִּי כִּי אֲדַבֵּר, אֲנִי עָנִיתִי מְאֹד. אֲנִי
אָמַרְתִּי בְחָפְזִי: כָּל הָאָדָם כֹּזֵב.

(I wish the Lord would hear my voice, my
   supplications.
For since He has listened to me,
in all my days I shall call on him.
When the pangs of death are upon me,
when I find nothing but trouble and sorrow,
then I shall call out the name of the Lord:
"O Lord, release my soul!"
For the Lord is gracious and righteous,
the Lord is merciful.
The Lord guards the simple; when I was poor He
   helped me.
Let my soul return to rest,
for the Lord has done well with it.
Since Thou hast saved me from death,
my eye from tears, my foot from stumbling,
I shall walk before the Lord in the lands of the living.
I have believed in Him even when, deeply hurt, I
   spoke
and said in haste: "All men are deceitful.")

The words could not have been meant literally. If "all who are hungry" had come in to eat, even if that referred only to people we knew, we would have had a small crowd: the ex-language teacher, a widow who lived across the street, whose sole income was a state pension that did not stretch far beyond her daily potatoes; my classmate with ten siblings — most of them male and endowed with voracious appetites — who never brought lunch to school (when I once tried to help her with homework she smiled a little sadly and said: "I'm just too tired . . ."); the sweet blue-eyed woman who ironed our large sheets for a nominal fee, who had been in prison a year for stealing a loaf of bread. (She had been charged with "sabotage.")

"All who are ready" to celebrate the Passover — I had never realized how many people were not only ready but eager to celebrate it, until the entire family went to the largest synagogue in Bucharest. (My sister and I were not told it was a "synagogue"; it was still too soon to be entrusted with such ideas, especially as it would have meant having to tell us so much more, and there was no easy way. . . .) Hundreds, perhaps thousands of people were there. No one moved, so as to hear everything that was being said inside. My family could not get even a glimpse of the interior but had to stand in the courtyard. I remember nothing of the building, because of the darkness and the fascinating impact of the people: their faces are imprinted on my memory indelibly, with the hard ink of shock and exhilaration. Strong, determined faces, thick eyebrows crowning angry eyes. They sang, too, and I so wanted to join in! We

53

were so many, many more than I had thought! All ready to celebrate.

At the time of our visit to the synagogue, I had not been aware of the fact that for seventeen years or so my father had always chosen the same day to go to inquire about the progress of our emigration proceedings. That day was Yom Kippur, the Day of Atonement, the beginning of the new Jewish year. It so happened that the purpose of our going to the synagogue had been to celebrate that particular holiday of Yom Kippur. We had never done it before, but suddenly we had a special reason: on that very day we had received our permission to emigrate to the West.

"Blessed are Thou, O Lord our God, ruler of the world, who has kept us alive, maintained us, and enabled us to reach this occasion." The words of the Passover feast had no immediate meaning for me at the time; and yet, even without knowing what my father was saying, even without explanations, we all shared the knowledge that we had our very own holiday, that the state could not — however much it wanted to, for the sake of public unity — destroy our private celebration; it could not deny that we felt very special about the occasion. When we children found out the name of our feast, we had already crossed the big sea, eaten lots of bread dipped in sour milk, and the bitter herbs were beginning to taste quite sweet. We learned about the prayers, too, and were not in the least surprised that the Lord had no name.

I must take this gypsy woman's flowers somewhere, give them to a child or take them to a cemetery. I think of another friend I could visit. I know her address, I'll just drop in. As soon as she answers the door she stops, stunned. A grave, a memory, a lost love.

It's late, after midnight. Ordinary public transportation is no longer available — I must take a taxi. After a long wait, I spot one. The young driver tells me politely that he must get some gas — if I'm in a hurry, therefore, he suggests I wait for another car. Of course I'm in no rush, I'm delighted to find him — the first well-mannered stranger I've met all day.

He's very young, probably out of school — he wouldn't be working "on the side" while going to college (he would need all his time to study, to get the best possible grades, in order that the state assign him to as good a job as possible). I ask if this is his profession. He tells me he cannot pass the university entrance exams, doesn't know why. I notice a plastic Madonna, and I ask if he is allowed to display it in a taxi. "Actually, they've given me a lot of trouble about it," he says. No, he isn't Roman Catholic; Romanian Orthodox. Yes, a believer. He was given this Madonna by a foreigner. It occurs to me that there may be many like him who are having trouble passing the entrance exams.

He asks me no questions but I sense a kinship and would like to be friends; I decide to tell him I'm a visitor from America. The shy young man now becomes totally silent. Is he afraid? Does he imagine I don't know I must be discreet? Perhaps he thinks I have forgotten the taste of danger; and probably I have. Maybe I don't understand his Madonna either, my pretensions to the contrary notwithstanding. We talk no more and let the night engulf us both, separately. I feel rather ashamed for causing him any alarm. When we arrive at the hotel I give him a big tip which he doesn't acknowledge—thanking me quite briefly.

The first thing I do the next day is visit the little church.

In front of our school was a beautiful little church, always empty it seemed. Strangely anachronistic, its Byzantine roof out of place among the ordinary apartment buildings, the church was almost too fancy, like an exotic ring on the hand of a milkmaid. I had often wondered what the church was like inside and why it was there, but for years I never set foot in it. Did the knowledge that I wasn't supposed to go inside a church hold me back? The apprehension that if I did go I would be found out and questioned by the Young Pioneers' organization? Possibly. More likely, however, I simply didn't wish to visit a building which according to my textbooks symbolized oppression and superstition.

Yet one day I did go in. The smell of candles and incense struck me first: inebriating, romantic, almost too strong for a place of worship. Along the stone walls were many gilded icons: primitive, even clumsy, but strikingly honest. (A nobility of symbol.) The silence, solemn but reassuring, defined the sanctuary's calm beauty most appropriately: to avoid intrusion into the believer's mind. This is his place; ours.

What did I know of this? In truth, next to nothing. The subtleties of the Romanian Orthodox faith were a mystery to me, as to my friends. "Religion is the opium of the people." On Christmas and Easter the school would organize parties — without music or fun, just gatherings with attendance required, designed to keep children away from churches and even away from home should some unenlightened, rebellious parent celebrate the barbaric holidays in some religious fashion. And yet this little church seemed so harmless, so peaceful, so sad. . . .

But who comes here anymore? Looking around, I saw that I wasn't alone: a woman knelt not far from me, motionless, her head buried in her hands. Never before having seen a stranger kneeling to pray, I felt slightly embarrassed. She didn't cry, showed no pain, didn't even seem to sense my presence. Did she take comfort in her prayer? Did she think the Virgin was listening? Perhaps the sainted Mother was answering back, saying something of peculiar importance to the quiet woman.

And to think that I was there as an ignorant visitor, on a "tour" like in a museum. . . . The icons seemed to scrutinize my intentions, tacitly inviting me to meditate. For an instant, I sensed a mute insistence — demanding that I make up my mind whether I would dissect the scenery with cold, analytic disapproval or else would let myself contemplate. Abruptly, almost afraid, I left the church, having decided I wouldn't allow it to reach me, wouldn't let the temptation of a peaceful Infinite cause havoc among my well-ordered, properly indexed beliefs.

57

Only many years later did I begin to unleash my mind in the silence of the sanctuary. On the campus of the University of Chicago, in little Bond Chapel, I started teaching myself the rudiments of listening to that compelling silence, to hear the heartbeat of the Sun. With no religious vocabulary, I couldn't pray; kneeling seemed awkward and pointless. But the music of the organ could harness the furies in my crowded brain and clear its skies to a familiar ether. If this be opium, the Harmonies work wondrous tricks to contruct the most plausible of truths.

On my return to the old spot I find the little church gone. It has been torn down, I am told, and in its place will be a new apartment complex: the school children are helping to build it by working during their summer vacation "for free." I look at the bricks, the frames of these new building, the dust, and remember the old church with the gentle icons.

There's no rush. I sit in a café near the marketplace, drinking some coffee. The sugar is dirty, as are the saucers, spoons, and tables; even the liquid in my cup seems slightly muddy, so I try to concentrate on the surroundings, the houses, and the passers-by whose gestures and inflections are familiar. Like it or not, I'm home.

A man has sat down next to my table. He's reading a newspaper. No matter—he won't bother me. It's almost reassuring to see these grim agents: the comforts of certainty. There won't be anything to report; my thoughts are drained of all hatred. The mind collects old images it fancied dead: the same small shops with those same painted signs washed out by rain and snow; the thirsty, half-wilted flowers of summer desperately surviving next to the hot pavement. I watch him from the corner of my eye: his grey suit a little large, his shoes unpolished, his thinning hair combed just right. He seems to see nothing, not even the paper he's reading, as if he doesn't really exist—only his purpose. What do big grey men know about coming home?

The waitress gives me no bill, so I must go to the cashier and pay—after she confirms I had only one cup of coffee. Originally, I had hoped to eat a roll, too, in lieu of breakfast, but the waitress had discouraged me with the assurance that the rolls in the window were hard as a rock. When I asked if she had any others she shrugged her shoulders to deny it, though she may have simply preferred not to bother: the store is state-owned — she gets a salary whether she sells or not, tips are illegal and I am too clumsy to attempt a bribe for such a small item.

Heading toward the market place and the shops, I hope for some excitement, although it's only morning: the interminable queues with quarrels and scenes will come later. I walk at a leisurely pace, observing all I can. The shops are empty, uninviting; no motley ads, no window decorations.

Come to think of it, the only time the stores had any color was Christmas. As the lights came on, Santa

Claus smiled everywhere: a jolly invitation to metaphor and fairy-land, reminiscent of beauty. It's hard to believe that in spite of an upbringing thoroughly soaked in hard-headed materialism even Romanian children have a Santa Claus.

His name is Moş Gerilă ("Old Man Frost"). He comes in a sled pulled by reindeer and looks just like his American counterpart, except that he brings presents on New Year's Eve and lays them next to a Winter Tree rather than a Christmas tree. The Romanian Winter Tree is full of candy, colored ornaments, candles, shiny ringlets, and personal decorations — except for angels, or any other kind of religious symbols. Nearly everyone who can afford it celebrates the coming of the New Year with a tree, wine, and dancing. Even the Jews.

A few days before the New Year my father would bring home a pine tree — much bigger than I was, and smelling as fresh as a forest after the rain. We would resurrect last year's ornaments, which didn't quite manage to dress up the tree, there being no more than seven or eight of them, so the big job was just ahead of us: making ring-chains out of colored paper and glue, and hanging up the delicious candy which came ready-wrapped in multi-colored foil. This candy would be eaten very slowly, one by one, throughout the week after the celebration; we couldn't demolish in a savage fit of childish hunger the painstakingly concocted holiday creation! My father taught me to make paper dolls, which proudly took their place among the ornaments, however clumsily conceived. Indeed, all my toys participated

60

in the beautification of this idol, as did every bit of colored or shiny paper in the house. No other occasion absorbed all my energies and devotion as did New Year's Eve: for hours I would attempt to apply my artistic intuitions —deficient as they may have been —to the assembly of our loveliest illusion of the year.

The traditional image of the Tree as Bride is altogether apt: we decorated our innocent conifer with all the lace worthy of a virgin, more expectant than midwives. And we offered this sacrificial gift to a groom known for his kindness and humor, a Prince whose subjects were the most loyal on earth for never questioning his divine right to love them. A ritual of childhood gratitude: the tree bore our libations to the gentle god of toys. Unlike the idols of grownups, Santa Claus had no two-faced powers that might benefit or hurt depending either on his whim or our servility; for his only mission was joy. And joy would come through make-believe, through the instruments of mockery of the useful and the purposeful in games adults played for blood. When on the fated Eve the candles were lit and the firecrackers laughed with gentle explosions, our hearts leapt for the miracle of pleasure, purged of all resentment and even, for short while, of all fear.

Not that I didn't know who bought me the cheap little presents that broke so quickly, for all the care that had gone into their selection. But if my parents saw no need to pretend, they also didn't insist on the truth; I thus engaged in the game children alone can fully master, of believing and not believing at the same time.

With the arrival of my little sister, the festival of

New Year was enhanced even more, since the family conspired to keep her in the dark as to Moş Gerilă's true identity. In fact, I created a whole series of myths for her, telling her about the remarkable territory over which he reigned. She was instructed in every detail of the gentleman's personal work habits, his employment practices, the responsibilities of his various servants, the qualities of his means of transportation (including mileage) — to all of which my sister added the frosting and the awe. Thus my small, unsuspecting victim was thoroughly enchanted every time she discovered the glowing tree and the presents miraculously laid in our home. To her, Moş Gerilă was not the mere symbol of generosity, fun, and hope, but the very King of Children. Above all, he ruled over a dream-world she delighted in, yearned for, believed. No Communist realism this — just charm and romance, as old-fashioned as childhood itself. She would ask me questions about Moş Gerilă as if I were an authority, an anointed messenger; such was her need to believe, she never doubted my omniscience. Her trust was both touching and intimidating, for though I felt guilty deceiving her, I admired her pleasure and even vaguely envied her ability to dream.

She was more than nine years old and already in America, a seasoned traveler who had learned two new languages, when a little playmate of hers three years her junior nonchalantly denied that Santa Claus had any domicile or reality. Determined to find out the truth, and sure that I would settle the matter, my sister came to me later that evening and asked softly: "Sherry says there really is no Santa Claus; is that true?" I knew I wouldn't be able to lie

The author's sister,
shortly before leaving Romania

*to her now, and yet it pained me to confess that yes,
it was true. My sister said nothing for a while and
then, her eyes lowered, she whispered "Oh . . . that's
too bad. . . ."*

My little camera hasn't been of much use; I don't take
photographs. My friends don't smile, and the buildings
are run down, having given up the air of dignity originally impressed upon them by proud architects convinced of inequality. The lofty embellishments intended to create an elite in stone have succumbed to the

rain which is collaborating with the new leadership in obliterating tradition. Their columns faded, wrinkled, old houses accept their fate with Stoic equanimity. Bucharest's facade gives way to the new crop of cardboard boxes designed for mass cohabitation.

The foreigner is invariably impressed with Bucharest, particularly if he never saw it before the war or if he was not aware of the city's rich history. Legend has it on hard evidence that the modern-day capital was founded by a simple man, Bucur, a shepherd or a fisherman, who built a little monastery on the shore of the Dîmbovița — the river that now crosses the city. The more prosaic historical record, however, favors the speculation that Bucharest had been inhabited for a hundred millenia, and was first baptized by Dracula (Prince Vlad Țepeș) in 1459. A portentous godfather.

At first built as a fortress against the Turks, the city developed as a significant trading and manufacturing center in the seventeenth century. Colorful names of streets dating from that time — yet to this day unchanged in appearance — reveal the mercantile turn in the city's fate: Furriers' Lane, Saddlemakers' Lane, Capmakers' Lane — reminders of the old guilds. One of those streets, Lipscani, was named after the city of Leipzig, where merchants from Bucharest annually traded their goods. Its many shops still preserve some of the old flavor, though, of course, they are now state-owned, thus lacking any variety or color, not to mention goods for sale.

The nineteenth century brought the rule of the Phanariots (Greeks from Phanar — the quarters around the lighthouse of Istanbul), Bucharest being still under Ottoman domination. This period saw the building of beautiful homes for the foreign rulers, financed with Romanian money. As commercial transactions grew in frequency, Bucharest came to be enriched by new buildings, notably the National Bank, erected in 1880. This was only a few years after Romania had gained its independence from the Turks. The nineteenth century transformed the capital into a truly cosmopolitan city: the Romanian Atheneum and the Palace of Justice, both French neo-Renaissance, are jewels in stone, while the houses of the time were modeled after Parisian villas and town houses.

With socialism came the boxes. At first we were duly impressed, until we'd visit someone and could see that each room was not much bigger than a large closet — a fact the facade ingeniously tried and often managed to hide. But at least Bucharest still had its parks — large, magnificent parks, full of flowers, complete with lakes and well-groomed alleys — and its large avenues.

Boulevard Jdanov is the most elegant residential area — each home a work of art. I remember visiting a school friend residing on Jdanov, whose father was a very highly placed official in the government: I simply couldn't believe she actually *lived* there — it looked like a museum. The staircase alone, meticulously sculpted in dark wood, bewitched me like a rare jewel. (This girl's family, despite such luxury, has since left for freer Western landscapes.)

I am told that today one cannot simply walk along Boulevard Jdanov — it has been closed off. Even cars can pass through only on "official business"; the visit must be prearranged, with permission from the host. The police are guarding the party's leaders from the people lest they ruin the sidewalks and peace of mind. Yet the result is also a walling in of the new class: a quarantine for the least scrupulous. Still the epidemic spreads, everyone yearning for privilege.

Meanwhile these dwellings live on. It's harder for the lesser buildings, more exposed to the public, to the defective sewage system, and to the abuse of over-crowding. Their inhabitants come and go, owning nothing as they move in, owning less as they leave. These homes, having lost their masters, are now orphans of the state. Just like the lovely mansion back in the mountains, years ago. . . .

With the help of a few enterprising mothers, our school organized a trip to Sinaia — as unusually picturesque resort in the Carpathian mountains near the king's splendid former palace, the Peleş. Students from the entire school were presumably eligible to go on this trip, but not everyone would be chosen — only the most dedicated little Communists and the students with the best grades would have the privilege of spending a few exciting days in a luxurious mansion that had belonged to a royal military club before the Soviet take-over of 1945.

And what a mansion! I can still see how it looked as we walked in: the statues, the fine old rugs, the intricately constructed chandeliers, all of which gave an appearance of delicacy, vulnerability, and un-shakable dignity. It seemed to ignore the invasion of a few dozen noisy kids determined to have a good time. Yet for some reason I was ashamed at having intruded. (Naturally, the political leaders would have found such a reaction inappropriate at best, so I kept it to myself.) I touched the detailed workings on the imposing yet comfortable wooden armchairs, and apologized in silence.

The mansion's old-fashioned beauty and sad romantic charm were bound to have an effect on the young hearts that shared its quarters. Our rigid, socialist upbringing had its expected result: unspeakable or at least unspoken fascination with the fluctuations of sentiment. A whole underground of desire and dream for which there were no words, no revolutionary meaning. Our leaders accused us of "decadence" whenever we laughed too loudly or danced too fast, breaking up our gatherings with a stern reprimand. We obeyed, less as a symptom of fear or cowardice than as a result of primordial shame. Those primitive urges civilized people must hide in euphemism truly perplexed us, even if not always consciously. But in the mansion, which added the respectability of marble to our wild fever, a way had to be found to celebrate our age.

The mansion's garden seemed designed with winter in mind: the statuettes and white stone sculpted benches echoed the snow rug that seemed to cover the earth like a mink-furred hug. As we walked, disturbing its fluffy texture, the snow came alive, sharing our steps and mingling with our carelessly chosen, clumsy words. Sitting next to a perfectly molded water-nymph on a bench of stone flowers is reason enough for adolescent eyes to glitter skyward: reminiscent of Renaissance midnights by some sumptuous castle dedicated to decadence. . . . It sounded so nice: "decadence." Meaning a fall, a gentle plunge, a dive into the waters of sin, its "cadence" the rhythm of wicked, erotic music. Love *was the mere overture; Saturn's stolen treasures were to follow, eagerly expected in the thralls of a first, tormenting, uneasy kiss, an uninitiated, clumsy, ideologically highly impure embrace.*

And so it was, as I examined Roland's eyes, steely blue against the snow. His large, warm hands in mine, I inspected them for tenderness, looking at each finger with the curiosity of a kitten on first encountering a new beast. How do we manufacture love? Eager to yield to the archetypal spell, fully aware of the new web we had been so willing, indeed so desperate to weave, we hadn't even learned to blush. We expected the web to mesh our common need, confusing our dreams long enough to create an all-consuming infatuation, the kind that burns up a youngster like brandy lit by match: a lively, immediate fire, slightly perfumed, too soon gone. At times we were afraid to budge, lest the mirage be lost or our savage intuitions revealed before the moon was full, the myth complete.

As we climbed the mountains near Sinaia, Roland and I chased each other like cubs, believing ourselves to be playing, unaware as yet of the forms such games would take with self-conscious adult lust. We'd fall in the snow and find its softness shockingly inviting . . . but, too shy to accept its challenge, we'd return to the chase.

I knew nothing about him except that he was a Jew, a fine tennis player and archer, who spoke both French and German and wore soft foreign shoes. I was to learn much later that his father's rare expertise in leather manufacturing had prevented the family from being allowed to leave for the West — their good breeding a not at all uncommon barrier to

68

freedom. Roland spoke little and he liked to look at people directly, attentively, scrutinizing their features as with a microscope. Most intimidating to a young girl.

At the mansion, he once played the piano for me. I closed my eyes and filled the room with pretty dancers, voluptuously lost, who floated on the carpet unaware of time or party leaders. Roland was dancing too, with someone who looked very much like me except that she was taller, radiant, and very sure. When the music stopped, Roland came up and kissed my hand.

Before we left the country, I gave him my diary and a few poems —items that could not be taken along, being "in writing" and thus potentially subversive. I never thought I would see him again. Yet we continued to correspond, and finally met once more: he flew to Detroit six years after the first encounter. We were both nineteen then. His family had eventually been allowed to emigrate, a year after us, and lived first in Germany, then France, where they had relatives. I couldn't quite understand why Roland had come to see me; already a veteran of several affairs, which he described in greater detail than necessary, perhaps he wished to recapture a lost spell —long since dispersed by the complacent elements.

He now spoke constantly, as if to prevent my saying what he already sensed I knew. His hair disheveled, eyes unable to focus on the listener, much thinner, as if inwardly consumed by inevitable hungry demons, Roland hated passionately, almost with abandon. He declared himself a convinced Communist; he hated the Pentagon, big business, the oil companies in particular, imperialism, profits. The predictable litany. His childhood training had succeeded: the equations had been firmly implanted, immune to new data, new variables. When he asked about me I remained silent, as if numbed by the apparition: prince turned frog, my fairy-tale metamorphosed into a comic strip. I could not remind him of the old mansion with its weeping chandeliers and fine rugs, the stately dwelling raped of its delicate dignity. His equations had no parameters whatever for it.

I haven't heard from Roland since, though undoubtedly he has blended in with the Western Zeitgeist, enjoying the comforts of shared platitudes, cheaper by the dozen. Sometimes I imagine him playing the piano in the early hours of the morning, mesmerizing someone new and lovely. And I remember how I used to watch his fingers attacking the keyboard, virile and rapid, to yield youthful magic. To me, his harmonies were quiet streams and busy birds, summer clouds and shy violets, promising sensuality so subtle I might have missed it but for my eager expectations. I wondered what he thought then as he was playing for me, whether his inspiration came from the same pastoral scenes, transposed in a key for us alone. If he had only played for me again perhaps I could have remembered him, his chords resonating in my nerves as before when it seemed he was touching them directly, manipulating the synapses as gently as the sea-bound wind.

All too often one starts to play the piano at an age too tender to appreciate the privilege of learning its mysteries. Barely acquainted with the landscape of simple emotions, I didn't anticipate that exotic geography of maturity to which the piano had special access. The drills were a chore. Enjoying a well-performed piece — that didn't come for years.

We didn't own a piano. This bothered me far less than it did grandpa, who agonized over it — he played the lottery each week, with exactly one purpose in mind: to buy me a piano. He had never learned to play an instrument, although he had an excellent ear for music and was able to pick up a melody on his harmonica or even on a piano in no time — building on it, composing, pouring his volcanic Hungarian soul into the tune. He would have loved to have me play just for him.

Grandpa never won at the lottery. Nor did he live to see the piano that my parents finally bought with nearly ten years' savings. It was a small second-hand instrument which a family friend tuned for us — testing each key, caressing the little hammers. It took him hours. Meanwhile we talked about music, and about him; I remember little of what was said but the impression stayed of serious concern for each note, as if a human organism were being operated on and mended for great tasks. If only because of the efforts and affection of so many people for my expensive toy, I practiced regularly, almost religiously.

With greater technical facility, but above all with age, there came the thrill of making music happen. My old black piano was to become an intimate friend, who helped me transform Bach fugues into romantic sonatas if I wished, who kept my fingers disciplined yet rewarded me with harmonies of my own creation. Often I would think of grandpa and

71

how happy he would have been to know that I had finally begun to satisfy his longing, however vicariously, with the requisite enthusiasm.

When the news came that we would be allowed to leave Romania, we had to sell all our belongings in a couple of weeks. It didn't much matter to me that we were offered a pittance for the few things we owned, since the money could not be taken out of Romania anyhow. But at least we hoped the buyers might be able to use these objects. Otherwise, all unsold items would be confiscated by the state and turned over to the privileged like so much war booty. One by one I saw our chairs, tables, books, and many kitchen utensils go to sympathetic strangers, friends of friends, or work colleagues of my father. These otherwise well-meaning people's cold, practical, almost shameless manner of evaluating our humble and faithful companions in everyday living proved to be more painful to me than the knowledge that we were being left without possessions. On the day the piano was taken, however, I stayed away from home. Something inside me felt the same as on the morning they buried grandpa.

In Brasov I will visit grandpa's grave and talk to him at great length. He must be told what has been happening to us — if he doesn't already know.

Strolling along the overheated streets, I reach Roland's former house. My fragile-souled friend had provided me with pleasant expectations. Like Romain Rolland's Jean Christophe or Hesse's Demian, this boy was the Sensitive Soul, vulnerable to a fault, in love whenever possible with the transcendent — of necessity at the expense of reality.

In truth, many of us do not escape these temptations of adolescence — the call to artisthood and sacrifice, vague images of self-denial and devotion to some Muse surreptitiously flying in the night. Not all survive the brief hallucinations of inexpensive grandeur accompanying casual conceptions and pseudo-creation. Fewer of us can boast of never having spilled our minds like so much spice over a certain restless lake to feign a brief immortality akin to godliness, if only for a few secret moments known only to the culprit. But we cannot afford to lose modesty for long or the body's natural secretions catch up with us and our shadows pull us back to size.

The house where Roland used to live is still here — as tiny and neat as ever, small gate and small lawn intact. I've visited it only once before, when he played the piano for me. We were alone in this house, it was late, getting dark, but I wouldn't go home — insisting that he go on playing, expecting the music to reveal another, wilder kingdom. As he played Rachmaninov or Mozart the cobwebs of perfection captured my willing fancy, so easily paralyzed with melody. My primitive sensuality was stirred to a religious hypnosis: the sacred paganism of a sonata. . . . I couldn't recapture that innocence today, whatever the effort.

I don't open the gate, there is no reason to enter — Roland is gone. The journey to the past might just as well continue. Down the street is the TV studio center — as shiny as a Walt Disney creation (on a cheaper scale). I could visit some of my old colleagues from my early "show biz" days, but decide not to do so. They are playing a different game; what could they say to me? The propaganda business has its price — talking to a foreigner may be risky.

The party line must be upheld come what may, intruders from reality need not trespass. The philosophy of the socialist screen is based on the unverifiability principle — the ratings be damned. Who can deny that the medium manufactures the message? The screen flashes truth by the pound — it's free of charge and nonfattening, the Five-Year Plan made palatable. . . .

No mere advertisements for totalitarianism here: the system was sold "no deposit/no return," the rehashed ritual yields new dirt in better packaging. God bless the packaging! We do the new labels with magic markers and indelible ink, typed like it isn't.

See the smiling faces smile. See the happy people sneer. No dentures, folks — just good-old genuine happiness. All five-year plans are created equal because all people are satisfied by all five-year plans. Let's hear it for the plans! for the five! for the years! for the equal! Equal in the eyes of the Lord! (Sabotage!) All right, equal in the eyes. The ayes have it because there are no nays. No negativism allowed! "We media people make sure the message comes through just as our Leader intends it: loud and clear and very positive. He writes the scripts, we edit." The editing is the hard part.

"Did you know that Hemingway died this morning?"

74

*No, I hadn't heard. Neither had the other actors
sharing the little bus that carried us daily to the film
studio located a few miles outside of Bucharest. We
were all shocked. Everyone had read at least* The
Old Man and the Sea *and had loved its simple,
allegorical style —a refreshing change from the
standard plots of socialist make-believe "realism."
Since actors were a privileged group — the able
spokesmen of the new religion — we didn't need to
hide our sadness (as we would have under ordinary circumstances, since Hemingway was an
American).*

*We were of course acting in a Communist movie
with some stock story about the people's fight for
Liberation. I played a child who wished eagerly to
become a hero in the bloody movement for the New
Order by participating in espionage and subversion.
It was fun to be dressed in rags and play at being
someone else, though I didn't give the part much
thought, let alone worry about not being particularly
good at it. Nor would it have surprised me to learn
(as I did, many years later) that no "Liberation"
movement had existed in Romania; there was no
more than a handful of Communists in the whole
country before 1945.*

*Being one of the actors had its advantages: these
were among the most cosmopolitan of professionals.
Between shootings, for example, we could retire to
one of the buses full of microphones and filming
equipment and listen to tapes of rock-and-roll music
which the masses were forbidden to enjoy.*

*We even saw foreign movies that were never re-
leased to the public. I remember watching* Porgy and
Bess, *without understanding a word, yet lost in the*

colors and lively dancing. I noticed that many of the blacks in the movie were well-dressed — better than most of us in Romania — and living in conditions far better than our propaganda had been leading us to believe. And then there was Snow White, *the delightful cartoon — I can hardly recapture the pleasure of watching it; never did I love a children's show so much! It was just plain fun, not another political morality play with clear (if dubiously ethical) implications.*

My days at the film studio, however, were not all delight and excitement; the tired actors, irritated and restless, would abuse each other as well as youngsters like me. In addition to the usual uncertainties of theater life, these people worried about losing their jobs on purely ideological grounds: the same game was being played here as elsewhere; outdoing one another in lip service, they hated themselves most. It was easier for an outsider to observe without sharing these concerns, yet the status of new adolescent had its own unexpected drawbacks. A young cameraman with a peculiar sense of humor took care to impress this upon one of the young girls in our group, without the slightest concern for her protests and embarrassment.

Behind the stage, then, the lives of these puppets that made our Communist theater work were far less simple than their roles. The flashes of capitalist entertainment were an added contrast to this ubiquitous insecurity.

Only a few weeks after I finished the movie, our family learned that we would be leaving for America. My first reaction was — would I be able to become a part of that unknown new world? Would I

be able to speak a language I had not yet learned?
Wasn't America quite decadent? From the little in-
formation that I could gather, the only conclusion I
was able to draw was that my new country was
unjust and frightening.

But the curiosity and excitement were stronger
than the doubts. I suspected that Porgy and Bess
may have been indicative of a different sort of liveli-
ness and optimism, the likes of which I never saw in
Romania: that dancing, so full of life, the people
enjoying themselves, was hard to dismiss as mere
artifice. Moreover, there was Hemingway; and the
old man catching his whale, who fell asleep dream-
ing of lions. No Ahab myself, yet fond of fishing, I
was willing to give it a try.

The TV studio was considerably more civilized and
less dangerous to the preservation of a young girl's
virtue than Romania's mini-Hollywood, but no different in essence — intellectual prostitution going on fla-
grantly, elaborately, regardless of sex. My roles on TV
were seemingly innocent enough: reciting poems about
the advantages of socialist economy and childhood
happiness under totalitarianism, acting in plays about
pioneers whose first allegiance was to the regime rather
than to their friends. I enjoyed being seen on screens
throughout the country, and being paid for it too. I had
hoped to earn enough to buy a record player, but that
wish never materialized; my savings were eventually
used at our departure to pay the very substantial fee
required to obtain the right of giving up our Romanian
citizenship.

The glamor wore off soon enough, however, as I

began to understand the masquerade. While everyone was steeped in ideology and we each had to recite the litany of the ruling religion, there nevertheless were degrees of necessary involvement. I was gradually beginning to see why the preservation of one's self-respect demanded that obsequiousness to ruling authority be kept to a cautious but absolute minimum, lest it dissolve the remnants of conscience. So I refused several TV engagements, and became a bit more reserved, observing and assessing people's motives more carefully than I would otherwise have wished. But most of the budding doubts I had at the time were put into perspective only much later, in America, particularly after reading Solzhenitsyn. His characters came alive for me, reincarnations of souls I used to watch wilt, sick with cancer of the heart.

I think many of us who have lived behind the Iron Curtain can easily sympathize with the pathetic Shulubin in *Cancer Ward:* dying of cancer of the anus, the guilt-ridden ex-librarian was fated to end his wretched days in a moral stench that had ironically become quite literal. After a lifetime of trying not to participate in the injustices around him, yet unable to oppose the bloody tides of an entire nation flowing at gunpoint against its own currents. Shulubin regrets his lack of heroism and is tortured with self-loathing. Not that he failed to understand the odds against simple candor:

> When we applauded we had to hold our big strong hands high in the air so that those around us and those on the platform would notice. Because who doesn't want to live? Who ever came out in your defense? Who ever objected? Where are they now? I knew one — Dima Olitsky — he abstained. He wasn't opposed, good

heavens no! He *abstained* on the vote to shoot the Industrial Party members [In November 1930 several leading Soviet scientists and economists were sentenced to death as "wreckers" for working for a counterrevolutionary Industrial Party. The party was, in fact, nonexistent. Their trial was one of the signs of the coming Great Purge.] "Explain!" they shouted. "Explain!" He stood up, his throat was dry as a bone. "I believe," he said, "that in the twelfth year of the Revolution we should be able to find alternative methods of repression. . . ." Aaah, the scoundrel! Accomplice! Enemy agent! The next morning he got a summons to the G.P.U. [the Soviet security police], and there he stayed for the rest of his life.

Is there a right to not vote? A right to not do wrong? To not sin against everyone? Against oneself? In Romania even children have to applaud on demand.

We all knew that sooner or later everyone, with the exception of one or two "rejects" who were constantly failing and would never amount to anything, would be given the pretty red kerchief of the pioneers. Nevertheless, some discrimination existed, based on scholarly performance: the best students were sworn into the Communist league first. For a few months, they would be the only members of their class wearing the special symbol. Next came the mediocre, and finally even the least gifted obtained their initiation badge, the "cravata roşie." Once earned, it had to be worn even if, as time went on, it was ironed much less often, thus unmistakably coming to resemble a dish rag. Some of us even began to wonder why our leaders considered it such

79

an honor and privilege if even the most disrespectful in our ranks were tying it around their unworthy necks. And what about all this talk of equality, if some became pioneers before others? Though our ideological upbringing had been advertised as flawless, we kept running into lots of confusion of this sort. Without bothering to resolve it, it was at least very clear to us that some in our midst were better, smarter, more likeable than others.

With this conviction firmly in mind, our whole class went prepared to vote in the election of the most equal of all pioneers in the school, our president. At any rate, we had been told *there would be an election. To our amazement, however, after the nomination of a frail individual we had never heard of before (and this was unusual, because we had a pretty good idea of everyone who was "anybody" in our school) . . . nominations were closed! At once surprised and outraged, we immediately decided to retaliate, however peacefully, by abstaining from voting. The unfamous (though admittedly not infamous) nominee was elected unanimously – unanimously, that is, except for the abstention of our class.*

Little did we know what was in store for us on the following day: the school principal, a tank of a woman, boiling mad, told us that unless we stopped this kind of behavior we would all suffer "very serious consequences." It was beginning to dawn on us that our frail president had not been elected accidentally. Mute, amazed, scared, and barely thirteen years old, we understood that we had been forbidden to abstain: there was no way out of partnership.

How can Shulubin run away from his own bleeding, rotting anus?

Just before dawn, I awaken with those violent stomach pains I had been expecting since my first glimpse of still medieval refrigeration in this too slowly modernizing capital. It must have been the eggs, says my mother; the salami, according to my father. In a spirit of compromise I suggest it was the combination, and urge my father to get me the next best thing to Alka Selzer this side of the Berlin Wall. Still half asleep, he runs out the door to find a pharmacy before my indigestion gets the best of me.

My parents and I haven't talked during the entire trip except for a few impressions exchanged on the street. While in the hotel, as soon as my father or I say something charged with *double entendre* my mother gives us a significant look as a reminder of the bugging devices sharing our quarters. We then try to speak with our eyes, in deference to our friends, who may be hurt by our discussions. This doesn't work very well, and since most of the day we go our own separate ways, meeting only at night before going to sleep, we are constantly frustrated, unable to communicate.

The medicine seems to help, in spite of its taste. My father sits down next to to me at the edge of the bed, watching for signs of relief. I assure him it's nothing to worry about, just think how much happier I'll be after I'm well again. He smiles and tells me the joke about the rabbi and the poor man who moves in with the pig and the goat. Not worth repeating — it's one of those anecdotes he has managed to collect over the years, ready to be resurrected for an *à propos,* amusing primarily for its remarkable effect on the storyteller himself. My father looks good for his sixty-one years, his eyes sparkle as ever.

Scientific Kaleidoscope . . . *The title was forbidding but inviting as well: a sorcerer's handbook? Pretending to describe little-known scientific facts and unusual learned tricks, this manual must have been dictated — I was sure of it — by some crafty witch who knew the workings of the devil. That my father could handle it so confidently (he had told me himself that he understood all of it), I found awesome. The book had been published by a respectable printer, and my father's name was on the inside cover. It said "Translated by . . ." which I was sure meant something like "discovered" or "understood solely by," because I could see that he had started out with some incomprehensible scribblings which he turned into regular words. If this alone wasn't magic, what was?*

There were lots of things that impressed me about my father. I could see him reading off some manuscript (originally written, he told me, in German, Hungarian, French, or even Russian) directly into Romanian, just as fast as the secretary could type. How could he read out intelligible words when in fact he was looking at foreign signs — nothing like Romanian — at that speed? *He made no corrections either — that was it, the finished copy. Sometimes my father typed it all himself, and did almost as well as the secretary. Watching his fingers fly on the keys of the typewriter,* "My goodness," *I thought,* "he can even do that!"

As I grew older, I realized that my father was working all the time — because we needed the money. With the extra income from his translations we could afford winter coats for me and for my sister, boots, meat every week, and even bicycles for each member of the family. It seemed to me that we were very well-off. But there was a price: my father had very little time to be with me, even on Sundays. Our family never went to restaurants, not simply because there wasn't enough money but because there was never any time. I don't remember having been to a movie with my father, let alone a concert. Whenever I think of him I see him working, always working.

But what was *his job? Translating was only* "on the side." *I couldn't be certain what my father did at his regular job. He was called a* "planning economist," *but the only thing he seemed to be doing was to inspect, seeing that people didn't steal things, and to make sure that construction sites had proper supplies. I remember he would often come home worried that the five-year plan would be impossible to fulfill without someone fixing the books again — the allocations were always widely out of line with actual needs. His title notwithstanding, my father didn't plan anything — it was all done* "from above"; *he merely supervised and was responsible if any-*

thing went wrong, if the buildings weren't getting built, if the allocations were insufficient. Since he couldn't revise the plan, it was quite impossible to win at this game — he was always a probable target for criticism and reprimand, if not imprisonment.

But others had it much worse. My father told us about the construction workers he met on his inspection rounds: working without winter coats in subzero temperatures, they lived in the tiniest rooms, and seldom ate meat. Nor was their workday merely eight hours long; they often labored into the night (without overtime pay, of course) to meet the goals of the five-year plan. Our family would give them old clothes that we had outgrown. One day, someone knocked at the door and as my mother opened it she saw a middle-aged bearded man, his shirt full of holes and his shoes tied with a string, holding a bag with a dozen eggs in it. He didn't want to come in, just handed her the bag a bit confused and shy: "We wanted to thank you, ma'm, the clothes — my little girl — this is all I could bring, these eggs — we have a chicken — thank you, ma'am, we really appreciate the clothes. . . ." My father later told us that the man had five small children. The eggs came in handy, for even when available on the market, at the price of about 30 cents each, they were limited to two per customer.

My father wasn't exactly trained to be a planning economist or any other sort of economist for that matter — his education had been interrupted too soon. While he was at the Commercial Academy in Paris, the storms of history interfered: World War II caught him by surprise, as it did almost everyone. In the midst of the war fever, unaware of the fate awaiting the Jews, he immediately returned to Romania, to his widowed mother. Luckier than many, he was offered a desk job in Bucharest that allowed him to send her some money. But not for long: within a few months, orders came that Jews were not permitted to work. They were also not to leave the city that they happened to inhabit at the time of the decree, so my father was "frozen" in Bucharest, a few hundred miles from his family.

Under these circumstances, his illegal trip to his mother in Brasov was not the simplest. It happened that a friend of the family was going to be driving to Brasov from Bucharest; as an officer, he could travel anywhere in Romania with a special permit available to all military personnel. My father's friend counted on being able to pass right by the guards, who, recognizing his uniform, would not stop the car to ask for his permit and thus not discover that, besides two women, one of his passengers was a runaway Jew going home. It was a gamble, but it worked. My father arrived in Brasov safely after a few hours of rapid night travel. The two women, incidentally, were the officer's wife and his mistress: they had a good, open relationship, seemingly satisfactory to all concerned — certainly, of course, to my father.

Not that his home would offer much protection: shortly after his arrival he was drafted for forced labor — digging ditches, shoveling dirt. He didn't complain. He was at least alive, if a bit tired. He tells me those four years were a good experience: now he really knows how to hold a shovel! (The first time I heard him say it I thought he was joking.)

It wasn't long before he was harnessed anew —

this time, to build socialism. Under the new regime, forced labor was called "voluntary work." At least one could take heart from the fact that it was being required of nearly everyone at some point. It seemed that "normal" times would never come. No longer willing to let politics interfere with starting a family, my father made sure my arrival into the world would be met with all the amenities he could afford.

In spite of my parents' worries and work, a great deal of care went into my upbringing. However brief his moments with me, my father inspired me with that genuine optimism of people used to danger. All was well when we joked or read or walked together.

I remember especially our favorite game: the squirrel stories. At night, before going to sleep, my father would invent the most intricate incidents involving a family of squirrels whose members were charming, daring, intelligent, and funny. Somehow I had gathered that the squirrel family was an idealized picture of us: after all, Mama-Squirrel made clothes, like my mother, Papa-Squirrel went to the office and also typed very fast; while Baby-Squirrel played with her dolls and kept getting into trouble. There were other members of the family who were less obviously modeled after people I knew, but each had a fascinating personality. All these squirrels could do what a Communist citizen would only dream about: they traveled anywhere they wished (even to the moon), they ate exotic foods (especially Swiss chocolates with nuts — every day! — like the kind that one of my mother's customers always brought us from Geneva), and they never had to go to socialist meetings. When my father was busy and couldn't tell me the promised bed-time

The author's father

stories, I would remind him on the next occasion:
"You owe me two (or three, or five) squirrel stories."
This meant a longer, more elaborate, more exciting
tale for that night, and a little less sleep for my
father.

I later learned that he would not have had to work
quite so hard, nor would he have earned so little,
even given his "unhealthy social origin," had he become a member of the party as he was urged to do
on several occasions. My father refused every time,
in spite of the drawbacks — like being "relocated,"
that is, transferred to worse, more grueling jobs
without being given all the reasons, only that it was
due to "ideological questions." After we left
Romania, he explained why he hadn't joined the
party. "I couldn't say 'white' when I saw black; it
isn't possible."

*It is possible, of course, but my father was not
going to engage in bad translation. He knew the
meanings of words too well, in too many languages — the language of sorrow, the language of
rage, the language of devotion. And what would his
children say? We still had lots of words to learn,
words like "dignity," and "truth." Papa-Squirrel was
always very fastidious about looking words up in
the dictionary, and applying them correctly. "You
know the joke about the rabbi and the dictionary?"*

My stomach seems to have settled for tea and toast but
I will interrupt my pilgrimage into the city until I'm
convinced that my digestive apparatus won't rebel
again. At least I may be left unattended, and my parents can start their visits for the day. It's getting to be
like going to the cemetery: everywhere we see ruins,
ashes. Hardly an hour goes by without crying over
someone's misfortune.

My mother is trying to figure out what to do about
her dress — it's been through a few days in the scorch-
ing heat, but she has nothing else to wear. All her
clothes have been donated, together with her cosmet-
ics, Kleenex tissues, even her eyeglass case, to needy
friends. We didn't realize how much we should have
brought along! Not that anyone is asking for anything.

The dirty dress will have to do, there is no other.
Anyway, my mother looks so good in it, remarkably
young.

*They nicknamed her "Little Blackie" because of her
dark complexion. A wiry little girl, she grew up in*

the medieval town of Sibiu, on the picturesque if dirty streets of the poorer quarter. She remembers little of her earliest years, but can't forget the time her teacher called her in front of the class and shouted "You dirty Jewess!" then banged her head against the blackboard. She returned to her desk bewildered and frightened, wondering what it all meant. Not that she didn't continue to love school. But at the age of twelve she had to quit because her mother couldn't even afford to buy her shoes. The shoes she did own were so worn out the soles had to be painted black to match the torn leather. My mother was horrified: what was she to do? Her childhood had never quite happened yet ended before it began, without any propsects for blooming again.

She had grown up without her father, who had left for America when she was barely two years old. He had taken along two sons and a daughter, expecting the rest of the family to join them as soon as he had established himself. My grandmother, however, decided to stay in Romania, keeping my mother and the youngest son, Bandi. As Bandi became ill with Parkinson's disease a few years later, he was not so much a companion to my mother as a patient, his gentle and understanding personality notwithstanding.

Going to school had been my mother's only joy as a child, a means of overcoming her family's twin burden of disease and poverty. Even after her stepfather's (grandpa's) arrival, the poverty was not alleviated, for as a station-master he made very little money. To earn an income, but also to escape the home atmosphere, as soon as she was taken out of

.

school my mother decided to start working. A few years later, they all moved to Brasov.

My mother was not the only one in Brasov who was frustrated and poor, yearning for an education impossible to obtain. Many Jews, sons and daughters of tailors, merchants, jewelers, had not had the money even to finish high school, let alone go to college. Many had formed close friendships, continuing to read and learn together. With help from others throughout her adolescence and youth, my mother read voraciously — on science, classical literature, and especially medicine. Her most burning desire was some day to own an encyclopedia so that she could look up anything she wanted, be able to read about everything, quench her thirst. As friends exchanged books and discussed them, they learned from each other, and sometimes they fell in love.

The war stifled these exchanges, since many were sent to concentration camps, some left the town, others still were taken to forced labor. Yet the tragedies also brought these Jews closer together, this being the chemistry of pain. It was during the war that my parents' romance first blossomed.

My parents were married near the end of the war, once they had papers. It was a brief event: after they gathered two trusty witnesses, a judge pronounced them devoted in legal affection. There had been no time nor money for a celebration, their parents were in another city, and anyhow no one could be bothered with tradition when it seemed that civilization itself was on trial. My parents spent their "honeymoon" in the hospital where my father was recovering from a pretended appendectomy performed by a family friend. The reason was simple: with the coming of the new regime, Jews were given the right to fight, hence my father had been duly drafted; afraid, however, that anti-Semitic Romanian soldiers would shoot him in the back, he avoided the army on "medical" grounds.

It might all have ended differently. Many of my mother's relatives lived in Sylvania's Czech, a little town full of poor, honest Jews with a good sense of humor and large families. On the eve of the war, my mother visited her uncle in that town, a tailor with more work and mouths to feed than minutes in the day. His name was Isaac. Uncle Isaac had said to her: "If you ever want to share our chala on the Sabbath, you are welcome to come and help me. I need someone, I'm getting too tired. You think about it." And he kissed her three times, with tears — feeling sorry for himself, or else perhaps suspecting he would never see her again. After the war broke out and Brasov became the target of American bombs, my mother didn't know what to do. Run away, illegally, to join her uncle? "Don't," said grandpa. "I know you, you'll work your hands to the bone in gratitude for the piece of bread they give you. If we go, we all go." They ended up staying. To this day my mother thanks grandpa for having saved their lives. For Uncle Isaac, and his big family, and all their relatives in the little town of Sylvania's Czech, were shipped to Auschwitz and were never heard from again.

On the other side of war, then, my mother was to be married, expecting to have a family. As soon as she could gather the necessary fee, she enrolled in a school to learn to sew, hoping in this way to earn a little extra money without having to leave home, *thus enabling her to raise her children herself. She was very much against letting others educate her children; having worked in a socialist day-care center, she made up her mind never to subject a child of hers to the neglect, indoctrination, and health hazards prevalent in such establishments (not to mention the unhealthy sexual behavior of children left unsupervised —incidents that horrified her).*

My mother was good at sewing; in the first month of training, her employer returned the entire amount

The author, with her mother

92

of the tuition and hired her instead. With these earnings, she was able to help my grandmother and crippled uncle in Brasov, who were barely able to survive on the meager pension they received from the state, which hardly paid for groceries and rent.

Yet my mother was not spared political complications. Even though she worked with her hands, she was politically an "undesirable element," a roadblock in the face of progress. For being self-employed was "petit bourgeois" — everyone was supposed to be working for the state. She had had to petition to be allowed to work at home, permission for which was given only temporarily on the grounds that she had small children. Upon our reaching fourteen, she was to stop working at home. As it was, she could only produce up to a certain quota, and her prices were set by the state — this in order to avoid any accumulation of private property. To enforce the regulations, a state official would occasionally come to inspect the whole house (unannounced, of course) to make sure that all the clothes mother made were properly accounted for, that she didn't exceed the limit of production nor charge above the fixed price. When my mother produced over the norm, she lived in fear of the inspector and trembled at each ring of the door bell.

Once in Paris, mother started to work again. Our friends, whom we had found without much trouble, were delighted to see my parents after so many years, and were eager to help. They gladly gave us names of people who could afford custom-made clothes. Not owning a sewing machine, my mother had to travel to their homes. But, since many of the women who hired her were cold and haughty, and

93

my mother spoke no French, this arrangement was far from ideal. At least it brought in some cash — nothing to frown upon, given a family blessed with six remarkably healthy appetites.

In America, mother continued to sew, this time with no limit on production, with no fear of intruding inspectors, and she saw both her daughters finish college. Swelling with pride, she attended the graduation ceremonies at the University of Chicago for each of my degrees. When it came to the doctorate, she wanted to hold my diploma in her hands. Never having had my head banged against the blackboard, I didn't know how many tons of tears and disappointments a diploma can cost.

A poem might capture her energy and vitality, her gentleness and generosity, the youth that captivates everyone who meets her. Words. . . .

I feel sick, I should go to sleep. After a short nap my stomach will feel much better.

We'll be leaving for Brasov tomorrow. It's just as well, for it started to rain in Bucharest and the sun has disappeared.

I cannot sleep. In part it's the heat, but also the

concern that each moment is important; I must see all I can now because I won't be back. After I publish this journal my friends will be even more reluctant to meet with me for (justified) fear of harassment; and I'll be afraid for myself too. Maybe someone will agree to come see me here at the hotel. Will A . . . ? I call the desk and they dial for me; my friend answers, very cool (though when I saw her yesterday at her home she had been delighted), and lets me understand it wouldn't be wise. Of course! how selfish of me to even consider. . . . I apologize, and as I put the phone down I realize that it's too late, her number has already been recorded in the government files. It's hard to get used to this, again.

Closing my eyes, I listen to the blood in my temples, keeping time, pounding at my brain. This doesn't feel in the least like home, there is fear all around me — it smells a little sour, like sweat or thin urine, and gives everyone a greenish look. The symptoms of fear are very easy to detect: pronounced, acute silence; protuberant, usually unsteady eyes with slightly dilated pupils (as if the light of day were a kind of night); abrupt, sometimes seemingly uncoordinated movements as if ready to strike or defend nothing in particular.

My room is cluttered with suitcases, wet towels, deodorant, postcards — hardly a haven for metaphysical speculation. I don't want to remember anything anymore. It would be nice to have a TV right now — I would even put up with some vapid housewife choosing between two identical brands of toilet cleaner. Although this hotel is one of the most luxurious in Bucharest, there are no TVs in the rooms. The sets are still expensive, as they were years ago when we first bought ours.

Our family was among the few fortunate enough to afford a TV soon after its introduction in Romania in the late fifties. With several years' savings, we bought a Russian Temp II. It seemed hard to believe that we would have entertainment coming out of such a simple box. As a very small child, I used to dream about having my own puppet show: little dolls performing on a personal stage whatever stories I wanted to see. But I never dared to hope that my wishes would come true so soon, so closely approximated! We would turn on the set about fifteen minutes before six in the evening, to tune it and to miss not a moment's entertainment. After the news came the children's show, before bedtime, watched religiously by every youngster lucky enough to own a set or live close enough to someone who did. We never considered wishing to have more than one channel — you can only watch one at a time, and besides, the party line would be the same on any other channel. . . . Indeed, we were more than pleased; our TV was in many ways a new member of the family.

Shortly after we bought the TV, we decided to inaugurate it on the evening that Beethoven's Ninth Symphony was being broadcast, and we invited many of our friends. They arrived en masse, *a couple of dozen of them, at the announced time. Barely able to fit in our living room (which also served as dining room, my parents' bedroom, and my father's study), we were close and cozy. The tea and cookies added to the party atmosphere, and it seemed like we were celebrating a major holiday — most of our guests had never seen a TV* screen before. The moment the music began, all the laughter and chatter died out instantly.

Among our many guests was the old Colonel, related to the three elderly ladies who lived in the apartment adjacent to ours. A refined gentleman from the old bourgeoisie, who now lived on a minuscule pension, the Colonel always delighted us with his French accent. In a nasal, deep voice he inquired into the small events of our lives, always interested in every detail. Of himself he said little, preferring instead to quip or to chat about some show he had seen, friends he had met. Invariably in a good mood, the Colonel had mastered the manners of another age.

So much the greater was my surprise when I noticed that, while listening to the music, the old Colonel was quietly but unmistakably in tears. Still smiling, his thin face alight with a peaceful glow, the Colonel seemed strangely young. Was it the excitement of our new technological wonder? Quite possibly; realizing that the new world was going on after he had essentially left it — or rather after he had been ousted from it as a political "undesirable" who had served the late King Carol and had been imprudent enough to have been born in the wrong social class. Or could he have been overwhelmed by the music itself? This may have been the real reason; the Colonel cherished music as a lover cherishes his beloved's letters and poems — we knew how he listened to nearly every classical concert broadcast on the radio, that he was a regular at the Symphony. He skimped on food just to buy the tickets; he liked to say that harmony is as nourishing as fresh cream.

Or he might have been remembering old times when he and his friends, perhaps a beautiful woman, went to the Atheneum to hear Beethoven. Why this handsome military man had never married remained a mystery to us — love was a topic he treated with both melancholy and elliptical humor.

In retrospect, however, it occurs to me that we had been listening to the Symphony of Joy, which exalts freedom, man's love of the sublime, spirituality embodied in human form. It would not surprise me if the old Colonel had been responding to the irony of that final hymn — unable to accept with equanimity the pain of the crumbled ideal that crushed him and so many others like him into impotence and oblivion.

I wonder if the old Colonel is still alive. I suppose there is no point in calling him; we are leaving for Brasov tomorrow.

The room is beginning to close in on me, and the rain sounds increasingly more inviting. I put on my bluejeans and decide to try the soothing baptism of the warm summer showers.

It's late afternoon, many people are outside in spite of the rain. Few carry umbrellas, oblivious to the gallons of water falling in streams, collecting in rivers on the pavement. Again I have the feeling of walking the wrong way on a one-way street, for people keep bumping into me as if their vision were clouded by water and fog. I adjust my perceptions, listening only to the angry, formidable storm.

Unscheduled, the rain brings relief: primeval events go on undisturbed; the elements haven't noticed the

98

anguish below. (Is Zeus squeezing some cloud, milking it to please a new immortal mistress?) Without really doubting the indifference of climate to human affairs, I recognize the appropriateness of the celestial flood. Tears and weeping are for simpler occasions, here we need a torrential outburst, an explosion of sorrow. The city is thundering its daily pain — the one protest that will go unpunished. Will it awaken the heavens? Or will it have to rain blood some day, just to be taken seriously?

Pressing against my hot, coiled body, my clothing has become superfluous, too wet to protect me. The rain has embraced me like an ally: it roars and frets, wordless.

Tomorrow, Brasov. I wonder if it will rain there too.

Rain came peacefully at grandma's house. A rather frequent summer occurrence, it was nevertheless a big event for me and my little sister. We observed the various changes most carefully. Sitting on the large window-sill among the carnations, we'd watch the neighbors rush by. If it happened to rain on a Friday, when grandma lit her candles, the drops provided a background to her prayers, akin to some timid organ accompaniment for a chant in a Gothic chapel. A white kerchief on her head, grandma spoke softly, eyes closed and palms touching, her serene face flickering by the weak candles — one for each daughter, each son. She seemed to be addressing someone she couldn't bear to see. The rain would make it all sound reassuring, and we suspected that God was listening, talking back with the drops.

We had always been very respectful of our little grandma, despite her petty fears and inexplicable loneliness. We didn't question her ability to make prayers real. She had authority over the flowers in the garden, over the poor silly chickens we befriended then treacherously slaughtered for special dinners, over the stove with its goodies, and over the candles. These were important powers, And she never abused our respect. Secretly, we knew that she respected us too: for our innocence and our uncanny ability to enjoy play, for our curiosity, and for the gift of youth — a gift she had lost too soon after puberty, to a mistaken marriage.

Did grandma ever teach us her sorrow? We sensed it, yet we could never understand it. Oblivious to the political world, her daily concerns seemed quite ordinary. We knew of no reason for her sadness. The war had left its scars, but the war was gone.

Only later did we come to appreciate her need. Grandma had prayed to empty candles: her children never wished to see her again. Those weeks when I watched her breathing through the metal hole in her throat, already unconscious except for her persistent, pounding heart, hopeful for more days — I realized how very alone she had always been. Her face was so lovely then, I couldn't really believe she was nearing the end. Her eyes closed, was she not praying still? Then one morning before the sun rose, the telephone rang, and as I picked up my extension I could hear the night nurse talking to my mother in a voice barely audible, as if unwilling to acknowledge that simple anticlimax, so easy to dread. As I put the phone down, I heard the rain and the rus-

tling of leaves mimicking whisper, but there was little question in my mind that the drops and the foliage had never listened to grandma — on that day or any other.

The rain stops abruptly, and the sun is out again. The heat returns with a vengeance.

"Grandma" — the author's maternal grandmother

My parents and I stop on the road to look at the mountains. Or is it to postpone the moment we shall see the house?

Brasov greets us with its least appealing quarters: the industrial neighborhoods, small apartment-houses lacking in poetry as much as in comfort. Further on come the centuries-old dwellings: we are approaching grandma's house. It won't be long. This is the street. The gate. The house.

We can't bring ourselves to go in. The two innocent victims of our exile, grandma and Uncle Bandi, had performed their uneasy symbiosis in this house. It had been their last stop before the coma. Throughout this trip we've tried to forget Bandi, unsuccessfully; his image is now before us and there is no running away.

Uncle Bandi's portrait is difficult to draw. Not that he was a terribly complex individual. Rather, what must be avoided is any impression that he was pitiful, or a burden. Paralyzed with Parkinson's disease for over thirty years, since the age of twelve, unable to walk by himself or to speak at will, salivating involuntarily almost all the time, Bandi embarrassed strangers and frightened little children, who ran away from his strident laugh. Yet to all who knew him well, Bandi's delightful wit, his incurable optimism, revealed an insatiable thirst for life. His eyes would light up at the sight of an acquaintance, and he would howl with joy when either one of us, his little nieces, would keep him company. When able to speak, which was seldom, he would tell us jokes or stories in that moaning, incomprehensible — though to us crystal clear — mutilated voice. He was our special friend, as close as a brother.

His eyes: full of spunk, modesty, compassion. . . . Having stayed a child, his soul a captive in its crippled, rigid, wasting carcass, Bandi had become all tenderness. The innocence and amazement concentrated in his pupils: why so much untold yearning, and such struggle? Always eager to talk yet usually unable, Bandi spoke the unspeakable and the self-evident with every fiber of that tortured, kind body he hauled around.

Grandma served him faithfully in spite of her countless complaints and curses. But all of us, including Bandi, sensed on apology in every curse, a desperate if clumsy caress or an attempt to forget that she, not God alone, brought this misery on the helpless creature whose umbilical cord would not be cut. So Bandi, out of respect and even pity, loved and protected her with his understanding, his company, his devotion, brightening her days with humor. (Bandi's rapid, very polished humorous style was enjoyed and admired by all who had learned to interpret his speech; since his diseased larynx didn't always cooperate, his punch lines had to be short, to the point, understated.) Actually, we knew that the bond between these two provided ultimately a kind

103

of salvation to both. It soothed grandma's tired, disillusioned soul, and it gave Bandi reason to love.

When they joined us in emigrating to the United States, Bandi was glad to come along —indeed, there wasn't any choice, he was completely dependent on us — but he doubted that he could survive the trip. While cheerful as always, he started having nightmares and would scream in his sleep, afraid of death.

We arrived in Paris, all six of us, my father carrying Bandi in his arms. Bandi kept joking, but the fear and anxiety had hardened his already rigid muscles —like so much brittle rope. He knew we were among strangers, penniless. And he couldn't walk.

A couple of weeks after we arrived in Paris, his sister, who lived in Detroit, sent us a letter: "We don't want mother and Bandi to come to the States," she wrote. "They must go to Israel." This would have been out of the question; the two of them could not survive alone. But why such a suggestion? Fear of hospital costs? We could see no other reason for her refusal to sign the required affidavit of support for us to come to America, together. (As it turned out, an American organization of the Jewish community, the HIAS, would have signed it had the sister claimed financial duress, but she said such a claim would not have been truthful!) We wrote back assuring her that she had nothing to worry about, that we would take care of Bandi and grandmother. But to no avail.

Winter came and passed and we were still in Paris, unable to leave. Knowing that he was the principal obstacle in our path, Bandi agonized. Then

104

came a new blow. At the health examination —a prerequisite for gaining admission to the States —he could not answer the doctor's questions intended to test his sanity. He was simply silent, and shaking. Too much excitement? Was he unable to move his lips? Did he fail to understand the interpreter's German? (Bandi spoke Yiddish-German, but not nearly as well as Romanian and Hungarian.) When he came home, Bandi was crushed, ashamed to have let us down. He couldn't sleep all night, nor many nights afterward.

Seeing that nothing was happening to change our situation, my father decided that the only way for the whole family to go to America was to have the four of us leave first and then arrange for Bandi and grandma to come later, on our guarantee. So eight months after we had arrived in Paris we left that city, which for us had been all too grey.

As soon as we arrived in New York, my father talked to a representative of the HIAS organization. After giving him a detailed explanation of our situation, my father arranged for grandma and Bandi to emigrate to the States. It was only a matter of time, we thought, for formalities to be finished and the family reunited.

Naturally, we were concerned about grandma alone with Bandi in a hotel, not speaking a word of French. Knowing that they would be coming soon helped, yet we worried just the same. Never could we have imagined, however, the eventual tragedy.

It happened less than a month after our departure from Paris. Seeing that no one had come out of grandma's hotel room for quite a while, the neighbors broke the door. They found her uncon-

105

scious in bed, with Bandi by her side — immobilized and transfigured with terror. Both of them were immediately taken to the hospital.

We learned about all of this only later, from a friend, Elizabeth Samuel, who happened to call on my grandmother about a week after the discovery, and was informed of what had happened. She ran to the hosptial, where she found grandma, who had suffered a stroke, out of touch with reality but at least alive. Elizabeth wrote us not to worry, she would take care of the two invalids. What she didn't say at that time was how she finally managed to locate Bandi. Since he was not, strictly speaking, ill, he had been placed out in a hallway of the hospital. Unable to eat by himself, he had not touched food

Uncle Bandi

106

since the day of grandmother's stroke. (He said to her that the nurses had addressed him as "sale étranger" — "dirty foreigner" — and didn't offer any assistance.) Elizabeth fed him, cleaned him, and promised to come back the next day. He thanked her with that gratitude common to creatures aware of never being able to repay the desperately needed help of a stranger; but his eyes were gravely tired. He looked at her with quiet disbelief. "Is mother dead?" he asked. Relieved to hear that grandma was still alive, he wasn't much consoled for long, doubting she would eventually recover. As for our family, we were beyond reach, too far to matter. Bandi knew exactly what was happening, his body unable to stop the throbbing of his nimble, now terrified soul.

Both Bandi and Elizabeth understood that she would not have to come to him much longer. Having been put in a draughty corridor, Bandi had caught pneumonia and died a few days later. This, at least, is Elizabeth's diagnosis. No doctor ever examined Bandi in that hospital.

Elizabeth revealed to us the details of Bandi's death only years later, when we returned to Paris once again. Bandi is buried there, too far for us to visit him as often as we think of him or need him. (I remember wishing, as a little girl, that all my friends who happened to die were buried in a garden behind my house so I could visit with them.) But sometimes when I am very happy and grateful to be in the United States, Bandi's radiant face comes to mind: he is celebrating with me. I hear his great, strident howl, his horrible, diseased laugh that could hold so much, so much joy.

Someone has noticed us. From the balcony on the first floor of the adjacent building, she is looking straight at us, smiling. "Mariana," I say, "do you remember us?" "Juliana," she whispers.

Mariana is a retarded girl, about my age. People used to make fun of her because she spoke strangely and could make you feel uneasy: with a scrutinizing, almost piercing gaze, she smiled — not obsequiously, but as if to reassure you that she would accept your condescension. She forgave her ignorant critics without knowing why she repelled them. We would see her taking walks then stopping to look at some dog, or peeping through a fence, or staring at nothing any of us could identify. She was fond of grandma and used to do chores for her, and talk to Bandi. When Bandi was able to answer Mariana was delighted, but we weren't sure that she could make out what he said — her reaction was less to the words themselves than to his friendly acknowledgment of her person. The language they used was essentially physical: two creatures society had shunned for being unsightly and slower, they kept a reservoir of affection and need augmented by the constant rejections they had come to expect.

Mariana is looking at us with that same intrusive stare. She does remember. Her eyes are peaceful, touched by an otherworldly compassion, as if she understood.

A woman appears at the window. "Come in," she invites us, warmly. She too has recognized us. "We used to live next door, in the basement," she reminds us. "There is another family living here too. We built a wall to divide the house — well, you know, we don't really get along. Filthy people, very. Separate entrances, yes. We broke the back wall for a new door.

Please come in." She takes us inside. We walk in, as if under a spell.

Grandma's bedroom — really everyone's bedroom after grandpa died and the state reduced grandma's allotted living space to one room plus kitchen — was full of treasures, each with its unique history, however small its monetary value. But of all her possessions, the wall behind her bed kept the most precious: a few dozen pictures her children had sent from America. She talked about each of them as if they came to visit her each Sunday for dinner: she often dreamt about them, and afterward recounted the stories, stitched together in her subconscious, as the literal truth.

But her children in fact wrote seldom and little, so we didn't really know what their lives were like. The censors added to our ignorance by confiscating letters containing "harmful" news. The most reliable information came through the occasional packages full of silky-soft, wild-printed fabrics, comfortable shoes with a lining that lasted for years, and tasty canned goods we ate slowly, wishing they could sustain us for a lifetime.

We knew next to nothing about the United States of America — why "United"? By whom? What "States"? Wasn't "America" the same as "The United States"? How would one distinguish America from its continent? Was the U.S. master of the entire (American) continent, de facto if not de jure? All that our high school history book had said about the evolution of this big nation amounted to four small pages.

First we learned that the Indians had been killed off; then little happened till the Civil War broke out over the issue of slavery. That issue, we were told, was never resolved and the blacks are still starving, jobless, deprived of all civil rights. Monopoly is the rule in the American economy: a few producers get together and fix prices, which are prohibitive. The "little guy" has no chance: the poor get poorer while the rich get richer. And, in America, money rules — there is no compassion. (I am told that even today the amount of information about the U.S. available to school children is essentially nil, and similarly simplified. Those with whom I spoke on my trip back cannot understand, for example, the concept of "welfare" even after I tried repeatedly to explain it. Why, in Romania everyone is forced to have a job—even it it means laying bricks or cleaning toilets after having finished a degree in architecture—or else be jailed for "parasitism.") At the shocking news that our family was to leave for America, therefore, I couldn't help wondering how we would survive among the greedy monopolists.

Once over the ocean it took a very short time to realize that we wouldn't starve. The New World proved eager to have us, to smile with us, to watch the new sun rise. But grandma's little treasures had been left behind, including the pictures of her children — the people who refused to help us come to America, afraid of financial burden. Although they had grossly overstated the extent of the epidemic, my malicious textbooks had been right about the existence of the deadly virus of materialism.

You knew it, when you saw grandma delirious in Paris, Adolph; you knew you had forgiven her long

110

ago. When you lay dying of cancer you told her once more in your dreams that you had been a good son who had written her long letters and had sent her packages of food during the war. You knew she always loved you, her firstborn; she still loves you and your family.

I hope she has forgiven you too, Bella, her cold nervous daughter. Your heart failed you in the end for lack of spiritual fuel, I'd say. But it had stopped so long ago of an overdose of bitterness and pain, it's a wonder you lived to middle age. Perhaps grandma had wronged you, perhaps she should have suckled you longer — who can say? You fought her to the end and then you both lost. She could have loved you still.

Grandma's children didn't wish to kill anyone. An innocence hangs in the American air. A dangerous, sometimes charming, but in the end very frightening innocence indeed. We soon came to realize that some of our new countrymen had too many walls to fill, with no room left for dear photographs, for pictures of another world.

The woman probably expects us to give her something. But we don't have anything, we didn't think of her, we didn't know she would be here. And even if we had, somehow we can't be generous, we can't help feeling that she has no right to be in grandma's house — an absurd thought. We must leave right away and avoid looking at those weeds, this disaster that used to be the loveliest, richest garden in the neighborhood. We must run out and never, never come back.

As long as we are here we must look up grandma's friend, Mrs. Blau, before going to grandpa. She lives only a block away. As we walk past the old grocery store (as empty as ever), we find her house easily. She lives upstairs; we knock, the door opens, and, after a few seconds of astonished silence, Mrs. Blau collapses, overwhelmed by tears. We look around the room: nothing had changed — the wobbly wooden table, the simple embroideries; she even wears that same ancient dress. We wait for her to quiet down but she can't: between sobs, she keeps saying "I've missed you so much."

After her husband's death, many years ago, Mrs. Blau had no one at all left but a brother in Israel. Our family had gradually become like her own — she brought us gifts, wrote us letters, and she tried to be a second grandma to us. Through the years, we wrote to her from America, admittedly seldom, and sent her a few packages with coffee, kitchen utensils, and a couple of dresses. "We were worried about you," says my mother, "because the package we sent you last Christmas came back, we didn't know why you hadn't accepted it." "What package? They never notified me!" We should have known, but can't find a plausible reason. "Anyhow, I couldn't have gone downtown to fetch it. I can't walk anymore."

She is still crying but she also smiles now. "My
dears, my dears," she keeps saying, not believing she
deserves such a blessing. Sitting silently, we look at
each other and know her happiness is too overwhelm-
ing to be enjoyable — she hurts so, in her loneliness, we
can feel the pain, we can't move. Of course we'll be
gone again — and this time, she knows, it's for good.

I get up and kiss her dear eyes. She reminds me of
grandma. "We'll be back, Mrs. Blau, we'll be back!" As
I run out I'm angry with myself for the parting lie, and
for bothering her difficult death with our futile search
for the past.

We are in no condition now to see grandpa's grave, but
this is a short trip and we must do it. On the way there
we buy some flowers. The cemetery is up on a hill; we
go in, and my mother walks directly to the spot which
she remembers to be her stepfather's resting place. My
father and I follow just a little behind. "It isn't here
anymore," she says in a faint voice.

The grave has not been kept: there is no name, so it
looks like the place has been sold. My mother puts the
flowers down and doesn't move. My father and I don't
know what to do — we walk about and we can't look at
her, or the flowers, or the grave. My father acts practi-
cally, to hide his alarm: he will find the person in
charge. A woman, dressed in peasant attire, is already

113

approaching us. "I don't know if it's been sold," she says in local Hungarian dialect, "my husband isn't here." Anyway, there is no name plate. We thank her, and she leaves.

We can't bring ourselves to just go. Grandpa never knew we had left him, he died years before. Now he doesn't know his grave is being erased. Maybe he doesn't mind. Do we apologize, secretly? Does my mother beg him to forgive her for leaving his grave unattended? We are waiting, somehow, for one of his juicy Hungarian curses. Won't he shake the earth and emerge to embrace us, his strong youthful body defying the long rest? Come on, grandpa, spit on it, tell us you'll come along? Show'em! We sit, mesmerized, hoping for a whistle. . . . My grandpa, my dance teacher. . . . We can't leave you.

It must have been very amusing to watch grandpa teach me the csárdás *(a Hungarian dance: two steps to the right, two steps to the left, followed by quick turns and a heavy dose of temperament mixed with pride): he, over six feet tall, me, a rather under-sized three-year-old. He would whistle the tune (grandpa had a favorite one just for us) and speed it up or slow it down, depending on the ease with which I caught on to the passionate* csárdás.

Grandpa's little lesson was fun, and even came in handy once. Our group of little three- and four-year-old dancers was putting on a show, and the teacher decided to use my "ethnic background" —I was going to dance to grandpa's Hungarian song. I agreed, hoping that his teaching had been success-ful. On the day of the show I was handed a costume:

114

little red shirt and little red bolero, with minuscule red Hungarian dancing boots. I felt very small and a bit silly in this outfit; as soon as I heard the tune on the piano, emotion rushed to my head. How could I get up on stage and dance there, all by myself? Then I remembered grandpa's powerful, protective presence, his gay whistle, his self-assured steps. No one in the audience knew it, but I danced up there . . . with grandpa!

A quarter of a century later, I was married. And, of course, there were Hungarian musicians to remind us of the past. Whatever the family felt about the memories mixed in with the traditional joy of such occasions, the joy prevailed. People applauded — mother with her charm and ebullience, the energy she radiated, danced her youth, her defiant love. Go on, go on! our American friends kept urging.

And we did. Amidst the dancing, my parents cried, though not for losing a daughter. These songs reminded them of their agonizing first years together, during the war; the lifelong friends, the people they lost to the fires. Then it was my turn. The bride dancing with her father. Dancing to the old tune that grandpa used to whistle.

I suddenly felt that I had little red boots on and the little red dress and I had finally learned to dance well enough — dance of life, dance of mellow ecstasy and chilled wine. . . . Where are you, grandpa?

It's getting late and we have more to see. We must go to the Jewish cemetery too. My father's parents.

115

The Jewish cemetery is farther up, on another hill, I had never been there before. Prudence had demanded that, due to my father's "unhealthy social origin," his parents' lives and the location of their graves be kept from me lest I ask embarrassing questions and become more alienated from my socialist environment after learning the answers. Rather than lie to me, therefore, my parents had decided to remain silent on the whole issue, and I tactfully refrained from inquiring into it, satisfied with pictures. (I would look at the yellowed prints a long time, trying to read from the faces and wrinkles the stories of these people's lives; from the objects in the photographs — the manner of my ancestors' daily existence. But pictures are remarkably inscrutable without reliable interpretation.)

We stop before the locked gate. A man greets us, and tells us we must pay $8 per person entrance fee. For a Romanian this is an exhorbitant amount (in real purchasing value, or on the black market, the equivalent of about $25 for each of us); we are shocked. They only charge the foreigners, he explains. Meaning, the returning Jews. For a moment we forget our grief; awakened again by mundane perfidy, we feel a little relieved from our memories. There is no point in arguing, however; the poor man doesn't own the cemetery, he too is a state employee. So we must pay for the privilege of

116

seeing the family graves. I have a feeling the man is sorry for us but is afraid to show it.

We walk along the graves, some well groomed, some apparently abandoned. Though Brasov had a sizable Jewish population — many of them wealthy, many well educated — the graveyard is small; a large proportion of Brasov's Jews died in Auschwitz and other ovens.

We come first to grandfather's grave — it's in a crypt, in stone, easy to find. We put the flowers as close to it as possible, though we can't place it on the crypt itself — it's too high, only one of several in the same stone wall. Next to it is the crypt grave of my father's older brother who died while still a small baby, as a result of an infection caused by circumcision. Today he would have been nearly seventy years old. He had been spared the interim turmoil.

We look for his mother's grave but we can't find it; it should be nearby. "I know it's here," my mother insists. We find a stone, it's overturned. I want my father to lift it, somehow I haven't the slightest doubt that this is it. The stone is very heavy, and he can't seem to budge it. When the grave keeper comes to help, together they manage. As they lift it, we can see the inscription: "Hedviga Gross." It strikes me that I had expected it to read "Grandmother Hedi."

She watches me intensely — steady, not serene. Her penetrating gaze has touched off a wrong nerve within me, confusing all my senses. I don't remember her face. I look at her pictures and try to rescue her image from the depths of my memory-case, but the early impressions are not sufficiently well engraved. Grandmother Hedi left us when I was barely four years old. She committed suicide.

117

Grandmother Hedi
with the author's father

Her death was not inconsistent with the life she had led — a woman of character, style, and imagination, who needed to preserve her dignity. After many attempts to transcend — this world, her world — she succumbed, unfulfilled, never having stopped yearning. This after two totalitarian regimes had confiscated nearly all she owned, had shaken her identity. Yet she kept her head high long after such a feat had become, for most, an impossibility.

Hedi had married young, at seventeen — beautiful, rich, cultured, yet unoccupied, and, like many upper middle-class Jewish wives, soon bored with her gentle but not especially romantic husband. So Hedi looked for diversions: literature, society. She was strongly attracted to Christianity and she later converted to Catholicism. Conversant with the most avant-garde European writing of the period, her friends were educated and interesting. Hedi was in love with learning and argument.

Her two sons grew up under her lovely, vaguely regal shadow. All the men in her life protected, adored, even feared her. But was she loved? Did she love? Her husband died when she was in her forties. If there had been little warmth in her home during his lifetime, still less would be apparent as she was widowed. I remember a picture of her — dressed in a long coat which she hugs tightly, she smiles while seeming to stifle an excruciating pain. Those who knew her well understood her constant, irrevocable loneliness.

Even so, one must expect that life had offered her some pleasures. Her friends, lovers, the devoted sons, an attractive home — with beautiful old things, replete with family memories, and little treasures cherished from mother to daughter—must have provided some solace. But the Nazis, and then the Communists, were to deny her all that.

The first fateful day came when the officers of the Swastika stepped into her home: "You have one hour to get out." What was there to take? Where?

She survived the war and the bombings with the utmost calm. While Brasov was on fire, explosions tearing at its heart, Hedi would knit a sweater or darn some socks, accepting with equanimity both sadism and the Divine Will.

When the Communists came, again she was left with nothing. A creature of another time, she had been driven out of her house twice too often. Without her milieu, without a reason for being, Hedi was wilting.

And then came the ordeal: the two years in prison for a crime not worth the name. She had kept a rather insignificant amount of money—about $200—in dollars (it was illegal at the time—as, indeed, it is still today—to own foreign currency). This after most of her possessions, worth many thousands of dollars, had already been confiscated. She had said that she wanted to keep a little money in case she became ill and needed private visits from a doctor—a poor excuse to Communist officials.

The prison conditions were far worse than she had expected. Locked in a cell with forty other women, without bathroom facilities except for a hole in the middle of the room, each day became more humiliating, more unbearable. And the most excruciating ordeal was yet to come: the prison guard, a lesbian, had singled out Hedi as the choicest prize.

120

Resistance was out of the question. Hedi's mind blurred under the strain, as she held on.

My mother, having left my father in Bucharest where he worked, came to Brasov to be close to Hedi during the hellish prison term. Twice a week, before dawn, she would go to the prison gates and stand in line so she could be the first one to talk to Hedi when conversation was permitted to begin, at noon. Since all the prisoners spoke with their relatives in the same room, it did not take long for the shouting to become unbearable. By being there early, my mother was assured of at least a few minutes of intelligible conversation. (The reason she could go twice a week rather than only once — which was the "quota" for relatives — was that she was given a special privilege by being from out of town.) Food could not be brought. Parcels were to be sent only once a month, through the mail, to be inspected by the censors. (Hence sending her poison, which she constantly begged for, was out of the question: the authorities would have found out immediately the source of the package, and my mother would have been convicted of attempted murder. This saved my mother from having to solve a dilemma that defied rationality.)

One day, Hedi told her she would love to see me, so it was arranged that on the following afternoon, at a specified time, my mother would bring me to the square in front of the prison and Hedi could get a glimpse of me, however distant — she was on the seventh floor, and the prison gate surrounded a large courtyard. We came at the determined time — of course I had no idea why we were in Brasov, that Hedi was in prison, that this was a prison, that a

121

plan had been arranged. As my mother pretended to tie my right shoe, she noticed that I was looking exactly in the direction of Hedi's window. "Do you see something, honey?" my mother asked, incredulous. "Of course," I answered quite naturally, "it's Grandma Hedi." My mother turned very pale: it was physically impossible for me to have seen anyone from that distance. "Why, that's silly," she said, and we left very quickly. The next day, Hedi said she regretted having suggested the encounter, for she had been unable to make out any of my features and it pained her to miss me so much. Strangely, I never mentioned Hedi's name after that incident, until we had left Romania. I was then three years old.

Hedi, shortly before her suicide

The years in captivity had nearly crushed her. Yet release did not mean peace either, for she soon got a summons to show up in court again. Terrified of repeating the experience, Hedi poisoned herself.

Did we mourn her? I wasn't even told what had happened to her until after the Iron Curtain was far behind us. No one really understood why she had committed suicide. Having been fortunate enough not to have perished in a Nazi concentration camp, having survived the war, how could she not have embraced life, making the most of it? Even in prison, everyone agreed, one must have hope.

But hope for what? For reading Communist novels and shouting slogans, parading for causes no one really believes, no one dares not to believe. . . . To Hedi, this may have seemed not quite worth surviving another prison term.

Having committed suicide, Hedi was by Jewish law denied a crypt next to her husband's, so she had to be buried in the ground near the fence. Her grave is not, therefore, as permanent. We leave her, uneasy about its future; judging from the fallen stone inscription, no one looks after it. But there is nothing we can do.

We don't leave yet. My parents walk along the graves, reading names. They meet old acquaintances and their children, their parents. A casual stroll, to an onlooker. But it occurs to me that my parents' generation of Jews was the most tortured in Brasov's history.

The evidence on the fate of Romanian Jews has come to us in bits and pieces, but the final picture is fairly clear. We know the number of Jews in prewar Romania was about 757,000, with another 150,000 Transylva-

123

nian Jews coming under Hungarian rule in August 1940. That same month the Romanian government started enacting anti-Jewish legislation: expelling Jews from the cultural life of the country, from government service, from the boards of commercial and industrial corporations; then, two months later, came the expropriation of Jewish property, and, finally, prohibition of all gainful employment. The murders started in January 1941 with a massacre in Bucharest, where about 170 Jews were murdered in a manner that, according to witnesses, defies imagination. But the first large-scale pogrom took place in June 1941, when thousands of Jews from Iasi were crowded into cattle cars, without food or water. Most died of suffocation — the others were shot: a total of about 8,000 died. Hannah Arendt, in her book on the Eichmann trial, writes that the Romanians practiced an especially cruel form of deportation: they would herd five thousand people into freight cars and let them die there of suffocation while the train traveled through the countryside without plan or aim for days on end. She writes, too, that "a favorite follow-up to these killings was to expose the corpses in Jewish butcher shops"; that the horrors of Romanian concentration camps "were more elaborate and more atrocious than anything we know of in Germany." Another 12,000 Jews were killed near Cernauti and Storojinetz, and over 200,000 perished in Bessarabia.

Another tactic of extermination was expulsion. Between August 1941 and the end of 1942, some 200,000 Romanian Jews had been shipped from Bessarabia to Transnistria (which was under German occupation), nearly two thirds of whom died of disease and hunger. Altogether only around 50,000 Jews survived in Transnistria. 50,000 were deported to

Siberia — what happened to them there, no one knows. What emerges from all this is that nearly 300,000 Jews had been killed in Romania *before* the Germans even got there! (The final count includes about 150,000 more killed by the Germans.) The history of German interventions to slow down the massacre so as to have it proceed in a more orderly and civilized manner is rather too ironic.

One final irony, however, was still to come: at the end of 1942, quite suddenly, the Romanian government discovered that it could get quite a bit of money by selling Jews: $1300 a head, to be exact. This is one reason why many people think of Romania as a "moderate" country that, at least in principle, let Jews emigrate to Palestine during the war. In truth, the emigration scheme did not prove to be particularly successful. But, as Hannah Arendt observes, it is interesting that the Romanian government was always "a step ahead" of the Germans: it had stripped the Jews of their nationality and had started the bloodbaths while the Germans were still only experimenting; then it decided to sell Jews more than a year before Himmler's "blood for trucks" operation.

All of this came as a surprise to my parents when they learned about it (much later, after we had left Romania), as it did to most Romanians and Romanian Jews. For due to lack of communication and the rapidity of destruction, its enormity was not evident. Moreover, as always, a government is to be distinguished from its people (even in democracies), and many Romanians had been very kind to the Jews. Many stood up to the persecution, often at great peril to themselves. For the most part, we don't know their names. But Ionel Perlea, the conductor, was one of them; he managed to escape and lived to give us more music; others disappeared without a trace. One cannot find fault with Hannah Arendt for failing to mention them: her book is a report on banality, the banality of evil. There is nothing particularly banal about the good.

My parents are now walking among the graves of those who had survived the war but had not been able to escape communism, eventually meeting their end in disappointment. Few of their sons and daughters are left in Brasov, most have emigrated to Israel. During the decade and a half of our absence, a remarkable number of my parents' friends died—people we had hoped to meet on this trip whom we meet now, mute.

I don't want to think about what my parents are feeling here, I want to go. We should leave the cemetery right now.

We are silent, trying to return to easier thoughts. I buy some postcards.

Visiting grandma's old house and the graveyards I had almost forgotten we were, after all, in picturesque old Brasov. As we ride through the mountains, I look back at the colorful city nestled within a valley, among rich green mountains.

An old Jew of Brasov, before the war

My father had told me once that Brasov had been founded in the eleventh century by peasants and artisans from Alsace-Lorraine, lured by the Hungarian kings to Transylvania through special privileges, in order to defend the border from invading barbarians. The article on Brasov in the Fifteenth Edition of the Encyclopaedia Britannica says that Brasov, on the contrary, was founded in the early thirteenth century by Teutonic knights. Since the encyclopaedia has its articles dealing with Romania written by professors who teach in Bucharest, I'll accept my father's version. In any event, whoever first settled in that lovely Transylvanian valley must have thanked his respective god, for the surroundings are blessed with uncommon charms.

127

For centuries afterward, the merchants of Brasov, carrying southward to Bucharest draperies, metal work, and grains, must have felt lucky to have been born so close to natural paradise.

Ever since the Middle Ages, Brasov had been an important cultural center. In the early fifteen hundreds, the humanist John Honterus — leader of the Reformation in Transylvania — founded the first printing press in that region, together with a library and a well-known lyceum named after him. (My father also attended the Honterus lyceum, and praises it to the skies: all his teachers had Ph.D.s in their respective disciplines.) The first books in the Romanian language were printed in Brasov in the sixteenth century.

Alongside the Germans, who were in the forefront of cultural life in all of Transylvania and formed a large part of Brasov's population, there lived Hungarians, Romanians, and Jews. Many had settled in the town as early as the fourteenth century, and each group had preserved its own distinctive culture. I used to enjoy taking walks through the town just to observe the different kinds of dwellings — most well-kept, with flowers in the windows.

The medieval Black Church near that market-place towered over us all. So-called because a fire blackened its walls in 1689, it was our protective angel, keeper of the city's soul. Grandma once pointed out to me a scuplture, on one of the church's pillars, representing a small boy. Legend has it that the church could not be completed for a long time — that the bricks laid by day would fall down during the night. It is said that one of the builders had a dream: the voice of an angel told him that his only son would have to be sacrificed, thrown from the top of the church. The angel promised that the boy's soul would then fly directly heavenward, and the church would be completed. The next morning, the builder, quite horrified, related the dream to his fellow workers. They all refused to believe him and told him to forget the whole thing. But the poor man couldn't do that; being deeply religious, he wouldn't disobey the angel. Thus, the following midnight, he led his only son to the roof of the church and gave him a push. Instead of falling, the child flew upward, never to be seen again. The next day, as the builders awakened, they saw no fallen bricks: the church had been completed. To honor the child whose spirit was holding the bricks together, they placed a stone statue in his likeness on the roof, at the spot where he disappeared from this life.

Its many churches and old fortress walls gave Brasov its unique historical flavor. At the same time, the different nationalities in town made it seem gay and cosmopolitan. I used to amuse myself by trying to distinguish the sturdy, quiet Saxons from the more fun-loving Hungarians, and both from the simpler, more business-like Romanian peasants. You could also tell who was Jewish: in a hurry, dressed as city dwellers, a bit nervous, their Semitic features often a handicap in those days of wide-spread attempts at emigration and the resulting anti-Jewish measures by the government (such as assigning very able and educated people to menial jobs).

Whatever its underlying anxieties — and there were many — Brasov was beautiful and alive. I notice that now the city is dirty, the people visibly poor, uniformly so. The old vistas are mostly overgrown with weeds.

129

The Black Church, Brasov

Some of the lovely large homes have additional rooms, built cheaply in different, anachronistic styles. (Aesthetics must give way to practicality. Tradition? An outgrown overcoat, tight and uncomfortable, not the elegant mantle of cumulative wisdom.)

"There it is." My father's face looks like weather-beaten stone. We have stopped at a spot from which he can see his home, that home twice seized. He doesn't want to go closer to it because he can tell from where we are standing that the house has not been kept up. It has died long ago, a few times; it is dying again.

We've all had quite enough of Brasov; we will gladly go to the mountains.

130

During our last days in Romania we hope to relax in the mountains; we take long walks along paths my parents knew well. The Carpathian vistas stretch for miles: on a clear day, the peaks reveal interesting patterns of trees and rock, sprinkled with villages and vegetation. Small brooks emerge from time to time as a happy comment, gurgling some witticism as the water trickles on stone. Yellow-reddish flowers behind a bush; blueberries. "We used to live on blueberries, on our trips during the war." My father likes to recall the excursions with my mother when blueberries provided sustenance for lunch and dinner. It occurs to me that we've been here before, on our last family outing in the mountains.

We weren't always fortunate enough to have both my mother and father as companions on a vacation, such trips being expensive and time-consuming. It was rather unusual, then, for the whole family to take a back-packing trip through the Carpathians that summer; sensing the extraordinary, I concentrated on the sights as if to photograph them inwardly for later recall. And, indeed, it turned out to have been the last time all four of us were there together.

We walked a long time, though at a leisurely pace, so that even little sister, who had recently come out of babyhood, could manage. We ate raspberries and blueberries, we drank cold water from the unruly brooks, and guessed what birds were calling us to play. My parents would tell us little stories — for instance, that we had just walked by my father's family home, the hiding place which kept them safe during the war — but the sun being too strong, the smell of flowers and woods mildly hallucinogenic, we couldn't pay attention.

I don't know how old I was before the fragments started to fit together, before I started to understand that our peaceful summer excursion, when the two of us little girls were eager to find berries and flowers, and to play hide-and-seek, was on the same route my parents had taken to escape the terror of war and bombardment. They travelled those paths illegally, wearing the Jewish star, without any identification papers, and in spite of strict orders to stay in Brasov, their residence. They traveled anyhow, to see the mountains (always hoping it wouldn't be for the last time), hiding from soldiers and explosions, refusing to surrender the years of youth and adventure to the absurd demands of some wicked war.

The paths have changed a bit. The explosions are silent and more subtle; no one wears Jewish or any other stars because the identity of every citizen is transparent: there is no escape. The targets have been chosen and they are everyone.

132

We return to Bucharest for the journey back to America. The detour to Brasov, like a brief hallucination, is lingering on against our will.

In a few hours I'll be in Chicago again, and all will be quietly forgotten — back to my daily concerns, the phallic skyscrapers, and CBS News. Who will believe my journey? How many of my well-intentioned friends will allow themselves a lucid instant away from their psychedelic visions of socialist utopia? Growing up in the America of the *New York Times,* how easily we become the victims of the Idols of the Theater. The prism of fashion and commonplace will shape the eye, crossing the nerves; it short-circuits common sense and the blackout proceeds to conquer all. The fall within.

My dear U.S.A., World of the Best Possible Hamburger. . . . The politics of catsup and potato chips has ruined our palates. We don't believe in the finer distinctions; government by The-people for The-people. (What-people? Us-people — yous'n-me.) The best-looking silicone-filled bikinis under the sun, one-way ticket to paradise all expenses paid on American Express, what this country needs is a healthy little pig in every pot. My dear U.S.A., you sleep so soundly your Sominex-dreamful sleep. . . .

Look in the Yellow Pages under P for Pursuit of Happiness — we cater to the Jeffersonian myth twenty-four hours a day, pursuing forever; we'll never go out of business! An Equal Opportunity Outfit catering to all shapes and sizes. (Have a glass of vodka, honey — no taste but it gets to you like dynamite: we toast to brotherhood and Wonder Bread!)

I've loved you so — vainly psychoanalyzing away your malaise, worshipping your own erogenous zones, resenting Christmas for ending the string of shopping days, dreaming in church about the sins you wish you could have committed and repenting for those you were too bored to avoid — I've loved you for not pretending, for displaying your mucus-stained linen before the stunned stare of the hypocrite in more frigid lands. The cream pies come flying into your face and you lick them off as dessert, apologizing for providing the cream and manufacturing the pie-shell. You clean yourself with your disposable tissues, disposable soap, disposable insult-erasers, ready to confront the crowd once more, rosy-cheeked and born again. I've loved you desperately, yet ashamed to make love to you lest you'd think I knew you. No one does; the facade is too thick, our politicians too ready-made, Madison Avenue suburban chic: they vote as you say and you say as they vote — a circle less vicious than tedious, interminable, exasperating.

I've driven along your clean highways complete with CB fans outwitting the cops, stopped at your white Mobil stations *cum* complimentary car-wash, consumed your pasteurized milk in your neat cup-size containers, traveled hundreds of virgin miles along preserved canyons and deserts — preserved from us all,

134

from the planned progeny of the pill with its impeccable ecological credentials. I've strolled through the sand of your rugged shores, perplexed and in love with your lonely majesty, immune from those who would know you by pollution alone.

And I've danced with thin, bright, promiscuous college boys who had thrown away their dandruff shampoos and fluoride toothpaste in search of that other America that never was anyway but it could have been — and then oh, my lovely, it could have been. . . . They hated your plastic cups and paper plates, your popcorn machines and portable catsup packets: such is the stuff of which wars are made. And still the popcorn machine wins in the end even as you lose the battle of wits, the duel of the commas and axioms. Out of the rubble the puppies emerge, licking their wounds and searching for hamburger scraps, oblivious to propaganda. What will we all do when we run out of hamburger scraps, I wonder? Grow vegetarian puppies and sip brotherhood for breakfast?

How do we unscramble the eggs? To think that only a few hours from Chicago people have given up on us and on each other, shouting slogans of unity while sharing bathrooms with "comrades" they despise. . . . My photographs are so few, and are beginning to blur.

There will be new pictures, but their very sharpness will inevitably distort, obliterating the events beneath. Our Polaroid precision dissolves the fragile veneer; antiseptic, deodorized contrast, too perfect for loveliness. The plastic chairs at the Waffle House are not for memory and frames; the drive-in movie but a larger TV-set, ephemeral as drive-in-drive-out sex and just as frankly histrionic.

135

Not that America has lost the touch for homemade jam and fresh-cut wood. There is still a Waitsfield, Vermont, where they know the price of a woodpecker. If Ralph Joslin is seventy-five, you'd never know it because when he boasts about it he dances a little jig, just to throw you off and watch your admiration. He still has an eye for the ladies but mostly for his own, who wakes up with him at five in the morning to fix the stove and feed Lassie. Lassie barks whenever anyone gives Ralph a hug — such is jealousy in an aging collie who is now reduced to sleeping under the kitchen table. The Joslins' Round Barn is for skiers, and has been for a dozen and more years, but it serves mostly as refuge from the madness that seeps in through newspapers and an old radio. The Joslins are mighty proud people who intend to leave proudly, dancing the jig, and they sure don't have much use for folk who don't reckon that's the simplest way to keep fit.

Skiing I learned from Roger, who first practiced on the hill behind his house in upstate New York. A little fellow, just turned four, his father gave him his first pair of skis and told him to put the hill to good use. There wasn't much else you could do in the middle of nowhere but learn to ski and love the mountains, curse the beavers who flood good garden-land, tell birds apart, and yearn to join the world someday. College? Not really believing that an Ivy League school would accept him, he nevertheless applied to Columbia. When the letter of acceptance arrived, he still wasn't sure he should go. He had little money from home, he'd need to work too many hours, take out too many loans. But college it had to be. So he drove a taxi: nights after classes and study, he would pick up his noisy yellow

Checker and hunt for passengers till two or three in the morning, in mad New York.

When I met Roger, we were graduate students in philosophy at the University of Chicago, Milton Friedman's home. By then he had paid for most of his B.A. in hard cash, and was now ready to support himself for the dissertation. At a party one night he told me about the time he was walking home, after ten hours of driving, so tired he tripped, his small cigar box of change falling on the pavement. He watched the tips he had earned that night spill over the subway grating into the bowels of New York, all twelve dollars he had hustled for, and he ached, then laughed.

I didn't have to tell Roger much about my own beginning here, starting without knowing any English, my father bringing in about $75 a week working for an old Jewish gentleman from Bessarabia who specialized in taking over businesses that went bankrupt, then selling their merchandize. From that small check, there was furniture to be bought, rent to be paid, clothes to be provided, dishes to be replaced. The fate of our dishes is still vivid in my mind.

When our trunk finally arrived, the trunk we had brought from Romania but kept unopened in Paris, we gathered around it for the few winter clothes, grandma's fine old china, a warm quilt. Unfortunately, the two movers, unmindful of the event, had dropped the trunk with such abandon that a crash was heard and, as we expected, most of the dishes were destroyed. Since my father wasn't home at the time and none of us spoke English well enough to protest articulately, the crime went unexpiated. The two men didn't stay to learn the history of the damaged goods.

The flight has been postponed for the third time, we won't leave till evening. A friend suggests we go to the Mogoşoaia Castle and retreat from the fermenting city — I accept with gratitude.

A few miles into the countryside, the castle is a true architectural wonder; blending Romanian, Venetian, and Byzantine styles, its intricately sculpted stone arches are still remarkably elegant, indeed increasingly so with age. This dwelling, formerly belonging to a distinguished line of Romanian aristocrats, the Brîncoveanu family, brings this country's turbulent heritage clearly into focus as a testimony to persistence and resilience in the face of varied upheavals.

The Dacs, the earliest ancestors of modern Romanians, had bravely confronted the Romans in the first century A.D., and succumbed to Emperor Trajan only after decades of resistance. Throughout the Middle Ages, the Turks were fought, often successfully, by Stephen the Great, Mircea the Elder, Mihai the Brave; their very names ring with the romance of idealism and popular trust. But with the exception of brief episodes of independence, some foreign ruler was always dictating Romania's policies and drinking its ever-plentiful milk. Not until 1877 did it gain status as a nation, after a final battle with the already exhausted Turks. (As for Transylvania, which flourished in the quite enlightened

The Mogoşoaia Castle

Austro-Hungarian Empire, the few powerful architects of the World War I settlement — the logical implications of which were not long in emerging — annexed it to Romania with no obvious concern for the political and economic complexities of the area nor the wishes of the native population.)

The Brîncoveanus' fate provides a microcosm. Constantin, prince of Wallachia (southern Romania), first established his residence in Mogoşoaia in 1688. A Turkish vassal, he defeated the Austrian army which endeavored to subjugate him in 1690. Like many subsequent Romanian leaders, he tried to insure his autonomy by being friendly with two opposing enemies, then attempting to deceive them both. While a secret ally of Peter the Great, he later failed to support the Russian tsar against the Turks. But the Turks, after

139

learning about the alliance, did not spare Constantin, killing him and his four sons in Istanbul in 1714. By then the castle of Mogoşoaia had been built. It was later reinhabited by Constantin's remaining heirs, one of whom was the well-known nineteenth-century schol- ar Grigore Brîncoveanu.

It is no accident, however, that the last bearer of the family name (at least before her marriage), Countess Anna de Noailles, a famed poet, flourished and died in France. Like Anna, many of the best Romanian intel- lectuals left their homes for less troubled horizons, for larger audiences and fewer political restraints. Today, the Mogoşoaia Castle is no one's home, a mere relic of former days, richer in imagination and hope.

As I walk through the ancient castle I stop to examine the leather-bound books, so intricately illus- trated, the gilded icons, sculptures, finely embroidered tablecloths (woven with golden and silver threads), the metal-laced cups. I listen for ghosts in the corners, but no one whispers a word: they have noticed the plain- clothesmen and won't betray themselves. I wink to let them know I haven't been fooled by such obvious silence.

As I complete my tour, it occurs to me that I am spending my last day in Romania paying my respects to the country's once vibrant, now dying tradition — much as I did years ago on the last day before the exile.

Our last day in Bucharest. . . . I was starting to feel like a stranger, unwanted, resented, lost. Most of my friends had repudiated me as an "enemy of the Republic" and, imbued with the same ideology, I couldn't easily dismiss this as nonsense.

When I returned my U.T.M. (Young Communists) card to the party representative, the response was, again, chilly. Didn't I know that I would leave? she asked, implying I had been a hypocrite in asking for the U.T.M. card in the first place. I resented the question. I resented, in fact, that I had to sneak away without saying good-bye to most of my colleagues, to avoid their accusations — or, as I suspected, their envy.

I was anxious to have this ordeal end, especially because of the possibility that at the last minute we might be forbidden to leave. It had happened before: Jews who had no possessions left, no citizenship, no jobs of course, would be turned back and forced to stay. We had already been told, in fact, on the occasion when the whole family was ready to sign the final papers, after ten hours of waiting in a dark windowless room, that we were to come back in three weeks. No explanation given. Irritated by my father's stunned silence, the official shouted: "If you don't get out immediately, you'll all stay here!" He meant, quite literally, that particular building: it also housed the city jail. By then we had sold everything and were living with the three elderly ladies in the adjacent apartment. Would we be held back? The nightmare of such a prospect continued to haunt my father, in his sleep, for years to come.

It so happened that during our last feverish days in Bucharest the writer Mihail Sadoveanu died, at a ripe old age. His body was to be placed in the Atheneum for a popular farewell — for all of us. It seemed altogether appropriate for me to go see him on our last day in Romania. So after staying in line with the hundreds of other people who had come

141

there to mourn his end, I had a chance to view his rigid, peaceful body. On leaving the Atheneum, I felt relieved: without a doubt, Sadoveanu had been smiling.

There were many reasons for visiting him. He had described his country as beautiful and wealthy, which indeed it was. He wrote of old times and the simple colorful people of the mountains, recreating the Middle Ages in Moldova (Eastern Romania), and conceiving many a bittersweet folk tale. His language was rich, careful, many-textured. Sadoveanu stood for much that I had admired and loved in a country that was, in a sense, going to die for me that day as it had died for him.

In truth, I had one other reason to visit Sadoveanu. He had once written a story about a little girl, Lizuca, who left her home because she was being treated unkindly and unjustly by her foster parents. She took along a little dog, Patrocle, and was headed for her grandmother's house when she got lost in a forest. Having walked much, she became tired and fell asleep. During her sleep, marvelous things happened: fairies danced, flowers told stories, animals and elves played games to make her happy.

I had acted the role of Lizuca in a school performance, the script written by my teacher based on Sadoveanu's story. But somewhere in the middle of the play I changed the words —I started to speak my own thoughts to the flowers, to the little dog, to myself.

And was I not Lizuca again, leaving my home with so little, and headed for the dark forest? I was hoping for dreams, for beautiful flowers, for a way to the other side. As I looked at Sadoveanu lying there, serenely, I wondered if he knew . . . if he knew what another side looked like . . . another side of night.

Back in the plane, headed for the United States. I had almost missed my flight: the last announced departure time, 11 P.M., turned out to have been wrong. At 10:25 when I arrived — a reasonable interval, I thought, to allow for customs — I found no one at the gate but a young woman, an airline employee. "The plane to America? It already left!" I had the sinking feeling of a prisoner whose parole had just been denied: a conspiracy to keep me in the land of shadows, I thought. Just to make sure, the woman went to check on the matter. She was back in what could have been an eternity. It turned out that the plane, though apparently scheduled to leave at 10:30 (which was already past) was still on the ground. We ran to it together, and as I saw the plane door open, mercifully lowering its steps for me, I could have embraced her, sighing with relief: the way to the other side was still available. Orpheus is allowed to return, for there had been no Eurydice to look back upon. Eurydice is gone, Eurydice never was.

I did not go through any customs check under the circumstances, and even if they had searched every corner of my small suitcase there would have been nothing to inquire about, no golden elephants, not even salami and chocolates. A hand-made embroidery by someone close, postcards of poor quality from Brasov, drawings of Christ by an artist who didn't dare show them to any of his compatriots. And yes, this notebook. They couldn't have objected to it even if they had read

143

it: as an American citizen, I was immune. Or I like to think so, anyway.

Fourteen years earlier, at a windowless police station, my parents and I had been crammed into a small room after a day of waiting (without food or water and, not knowing when our turn would come, unable to leave), then told to raise our hands for swearing. Reluctantly, I did as ordered. The oath was never to do anything that would harm the interests of the Romanian People's Republic. I said yes, as did my parents, but hesitated: whose interests were we talking about? The interests of this little man who had shouted at us three weeks ago, telling us to go home, without explaining the delay? The interests of the tight-lipped Young Communist party representative? Or the interests of sick old Mrs. Blau? Of the three old ladies who gave us one last shelter? I sensed that I had sworn a senseless, impossible oath which I had no intention of breaking, but that the little man who had never learned to smile would never be able to understand such a thing.

The plane finally started to move, ready for that moment of lightness when the breath stops and the new sound, sky-sound, suspends you in the complete if temporary illusion that earth is quite unnecessary, that you could live forever inside the womb of dusk. There; free again.

As I close my eyes I try to erase everything: the taxi-driver, the raspberries, the graves. But I'm never very successful at these exercises; the mind takes over quickly, and I find myself caught once again, the victim of some dream, as helpless as a fly inside a spider's web — except for the additional frustration resulting from the illusion that the web is my own and thus quite expendable. Yet this time I truly cannot say that I wish

144

to resist: for what I see before me, as persistent as the night, is a picture as serene as a little flower.

I used to look at her in a trance: a small girl, with a white ribbon in her hair, unsmiling yet perfectly calm, as if she alone could set straight any controversy or unnecessary disturbance. Her shoes spotlessly white, she sat on her chair holding my father's hand. I had never met her: in the picture, my father was only four years old. Her name was Marcia Kovatch, and she was his cousin. I was never to meet her because she had lost her life at Auschwitz. They gassed her, pregnant, in 1941. She was the same age I am today: twenty-eight.

It had always seemed to me that in the little girl's eyes there was a premonition, and resignation, peace. But it seemed, too, that she would have liked to say something from her picture, and if I only looked long enough I could hear it, read it, and tell it to everyone who cared to know. Maybe she was trying to tell us something very simple, as she held my father's hand: take care of him, he is a good little fellow, take care. Or maybe she was staring at us all, the people who survived her, and quietly wondered why she had been chosen, so young, for an end no one will ever understand.

But as her picture reappeared before my mind once more, I thought I could see her beginning to smile. It was not a happy smile, and it didn't really make me glad, but I felt that she was somehow with me, in the plane. And at the same time I remembered that my grandmother had told us, after she recovered for a brief time from her stroke, that what had really saved her in Paris was . . . grandpa's constant presence next to her. She never once doubted that grandpa, who had died six years earlier, had been with her, seeing to it that she

145

recovered, seeing to it that the doctors took good care of her. "We talked about everything," she said. Blissful lunacy, or true? I am prepared to believe. And so I was prepared to imagine Marcia next to me, within me, smiling as she talked softly, without moving her lips, to no one but myself. She said, as I would have expected, to take care. To remember how much shorter each day becomes, and how long the night is. But she also said that I shouldn't think about the night too much: there are many sides to it, and not all are frightful. "But there is one side . . ." I think I said, aloud.

I opened my eyes. No one had moved. Maybe I hadn't said anything. In any case, Marcia was gone, and instead I saw stars. Those stars have been there for millions of years . . . millions of stars. . . . Maybe on one of these stars lives Marcia. And on another star, Bandi. And grandma; grandpa. . . . Maybe the stars for the innocent are the ones that shine.

146

About the Author

Dr. Juliana Geran Pilon is director of the Center for Culture and Security and faculty chairman at the Institute of World Politics in Washington, D.C. Her other books include *Soulmates: Resurrecting Eve* (2011), *Cultural Intelligence for Winning the Peace* (2009), *Why America is Such a Hard Sell: Beyond Pride and Prejudice* (2007), *Every Vote Counts: The Role of Elections in Building Democracy,* co-edited with Richard Soudriette (2007), and *The Bloody Flag: Post-Communist Nationalism in Eastern Europe—Spotlight on Romania* (1992). Her anthology on civic education, *Ironic Points of Light,* was published in Estonian and Russian in 1998. She has also helped write and edit a textbook on civic education used, in country-specific versions, throughout Kazakhstan, Kyrgyzstan, and Tajikistan, endorsed by the departments of education in these countries. She has published over two hundred articles and reviews on international affairs, human rights, literature, and philosophy, and has made frequent appearances on the radio and television.

During the 1990s, she was first the director and later the vice president for programs at IFES, where she designed, conducted, and managed projects related to a wide variety of democratization projects. Born in Romania, she emigrated with her family and arrived in the U.S. as a teenager. After receiving her Ph.D. in philosophy from the University of Chicago, she held post-doctoral fellowships in international relations at Stanford University's Hoover Institution and at the Institute of Humane Studies. She has taught at several universities, including National Defense University, Air University's Language and Culture Center, Emory University, St. Mary's College of Maryland, Johns Hopkins, George Washington University, American University, and Rochester Institute of Technology. She is a member of the Council on Foreign Affairs and has served on the board of advisors of the Auschwitz-based human rights organization Oswiencim Institute for Human Rights and the International Advisory Board of B'nai Brith.